Mary Hartwell Catherwood

The spirit of an Illinois town, and The little Renault

Two stories of Illinois at different periods

Mary Hartwell Catherwood

The spirit of an Illinois town, and The little Renault
Two stories of Illinois at different periods

ISBN/EAN: 9783742891518

Manufactured in Europe, USA, Canada, Australia, Japa

Cover: Foto ©Thomas Meinert / pixelio.de

Manufactured and distributed by brebook publishing software
(www.brebook.com)

Mary Hartwell Catherwood

The spirit of an Illinois town, and The little Renault

THE SPIRIT OF AN ILLINOIS TOWN

AND

THE LITTLE RENAULT

TWO STORIES OF ILLINOIS
AT DIFFERENT
PERIODS
BY

MARY HARTWELL CATHERWOOD

WITH ILLUSTRATIONS

BOSTON AND NEW YORK
HOUGHTON, MIFFLIN AND COMPANY
The Riverside Press, Cambridge
1897

CONTENTS.

THE SPIRIT
OF AN ILLINOIS TOWN.

THE SPIRIT OF AN ILLINOIS TOWN.

I.

ON THE NORTH SIDE.

THE prairie was intersected by two rail-roads, and at their junction, without a single natural advantage, the town sprang up. Neither lake nor stream, neither old woods nor diversity of hills, lured man's enterprise to the spot; nothing but the bald rolling prairie, gorgeous, if you rode into its distances, with scarlet bunches of paint-lady, small yellow sunflowers, and lavender asters, and acres of other blooms. In yet undrained slews the iris flags stood in ranks, and at a passing touch millions of sensitive-plants folded their lace leaves and closed their black - eyed maize - colored blossoms. By such tokens it was early autumn the first evening Sam Peevey and I walked north along one of the principal streets to our new boarding-house.

We had begun by sleeping on benches provided for visiting subscribers in the sanctum of our new paper, and eating crackers and cheese and such cheap browse as the restaurants afforded. Sam was proud of this, and intended to put it in his future political speeches. As for me, I was ready for anything at that time. But our newspaper had so prospered that we could now afford to live in a house, and pay a woman who kept no other guests a modest price for boarding us.

Our belongings had already been sent to her care, and we hoped the drayload would impress her. Sam did the partnership hoping, for I did n't care for anything in the world. The street along which we walked to our new experiences had been a Pottawatomie trail from the Great Lakes; and mindful of bygones, the founders of the town called it on their map Trail Street.

Further justice had been done the Potta-watomies, and their forerunner in path-mak-ing, the buffalo, by naming the town Trail City. Long gaps of vacant lots still showed between buildings. Shopping women had to walk half a mile from the north side to the south side, matching samples. It was the favorite joke of merchants in this direction to bid their customers, "Give us a call on your way to Chicago." Some still thought the supremacy of trade might be wrested from Main Street on the south side, but others were wavering toward that thorough-fare. On every hand were scattering houses, from mansions having their own gas, and their water propelled by gayly painted wind-mills, to the rudest shelters of pine, in which lot-owners tabernacled until they could do better; every man's first care being to secure what promised to be the most valu-able location he could command.

Resin weed, strung with lumps of trans-lucent gum, brushed our knees at the edge of the sidewalk, which like a narrow endless bridge carried us above the black soil. This causeway let directly into many front rooms where the functions of humble life went on almost in public. But the virgin town was still untainted with deep poverty or vice. It had kept itself entirely free, Sam informed me, from that American institution called the saloon, so different from foreign wineshops. We were literally walking through a square mile of Ohio cheer, New England thrift and conscientiousness, Kentucky hospitality, New York far-sightedness with capital to back it, and native Illinois grit. The very air, resinous and sweet, had a peculiar tingle that a man, having once felt, cannot forget. Everybody was going to succeed, and on the way could put up with a few inconveniences.

The sun, a plainly defined ball, was melting away in its own radiance, and flattening as it melted, just above the horizon. This unobstructed setting made weird and long-shadowed effects. I hung back to see it touch ground beyond low buildings. Now

it was half gone — now three quarters; now
it was a disk of gold — a quivering thread
of fire — and now a memory. The wan-
ness of sudden twilight stole eastward. The
whole wide land was a map. A freight-
train trailed off into glorified northern prairie. The town-herder was bringing cows
out of the west, and we could hear farmers'
wagons rattling home on the dry autumnal
plain. Everybody wore a satisfied grin, because the days of rattlesnake-fighting were
over and a long-looked-for millennium had
come. Eastward, on a billow of the prairie,
a land agent with his swarm of followers
could be seen offering lots. Under the
clang of locomotive bells and the scattered
noises of a skeleton corporation came the
suction hint of the note of the bull-goose or
thunder-pumper, like a buried village working its pumps.

There were a great many passers, for
people were continually walking about to
gloat over the promised land, and brag, —
north side, south side, or west side; the

southwest quarter did not count, being re-
served for driving-parks, manufactories, and
other municipal appendages.

Sam was always in a hurry, but he let me
see the sunset as a spectacle of local value.
Sam was broad and pink and muscular.
He had been the athlete of our class, while
I was only the poor fellow who carried off
college honors. He intended to go in for
politics from the ground up. Congress was
one of his goals. Congress indorsed you for
the presidency, or any other job that came
your way after you had been elected town
alderman. Sam put a great deal of time
into what he called making himself solid
with people and left me to do the office
work, but I did n't want to be solid with
people. The only endearing characteristic
of the town was its Americanness. The
raw land, the unfinish, the glad rush, the
high, clear air, the jolly insolence of inde-
pendent human beings, — how American
they all were! I had been so sick for
things American. In Paris it had seemed

impossible to wait until the ship ferried me over. Gorgeous autumn colors of my country, high zenith shining as no other sky shines, clean gladness of a landscape unsoaked by mediæval filth, primitive still, but full of promise that no words can set forth, — my God! how my soul shouted hallelujah, while I whizzed through in a dining-car, paying five prices for a vile breakfast and rancid butter! If a man could always be coming home from Europe, he might accomplish something by the mere rise of his spirits. That was when I thought I could begin again where I had left off six years before.

"I'm hungry," said Sam. "And we're going to the house of one of the best amateur cooks in Trail City. But they say she has a falling jaw, and we don't want to let it drop on us. She's a holy terror over poor Kate Keene. Why don't you limber up, Seth, and fascinate folks as you used to before you went abroad? Travel's taken all the life out of you. Six years more of Europe would have made you an imbecile."

" Who 's Kate Keene ? "

" You did n't need six years more ; you 're an imbecile now. Ever since you dumped your baggage in Trail City and walked into the ' War Path ' office, you 've had the names of all the inhabitants put at your pen's end. Who 's Colonel York? Who 's Banker Babcock? I 'll make you a little catechism."

" You 'll make me an apology. You are taking an unpopular manner with me, and may lose my vote."

" Try to feel a little interest in humanity around you, Seth," pleaded Sam. " When Esther comes into the office to scrub, you do take her boy on your knee, and notice her and even her confounded crane."

" Esther comes only once a month. If we could afford to have her oftener, it might exhaust me."

" I tell you it is n't liked, Seth."

I laughed because he could think that would make any difference to me.

" Some of the finest families in the United

States have gathered to this town," blustered Sam. "Lucia and Alice York and Teresa Babcock, — where will you find prettier girls? And if you look at externals, there 'll be plenty of people sitting down to well-served dinners when we sit down to supper."

"I don't look at externals."

"I wish you did. For a fellow that works like a horse, you take confounded little notice of what's around you. Now, we ought to be laying our plans to get hold of some of this land while it's comparatively cheap. It 'll be worth a hundred dollars an acre some time. Rich, black, deep" —

" Up to a man's knees," said I.

" Or a mule's," assented Sam. " And we want some. You had a fortune when you left college." He gave me that cast of the eye with which he always approached this subject. It was almost a compensation to me for the loss of my fortune to see how defrauded Sam felt.

"If I had it now, would I be here?"

" But how could you run through with it
— all ? "

" Same old way."

" You had fifty thousand dollars."

" And you 'll come back at me fifty thousand times to make me account for every
dollar of it."

" You ought to account to somebody."

" That 's been one of my fatal troubles,
Sam : there was no one for me to account
to, — no father, mother, brother, or sister."

" I 'd be a brother to you and show you
where to put it now, if you had it. I don't
understand how you let foreigners rob you
so ; you 're no profligate. Buying old books
and old pictures is n't absolute drunkenness."

I never excused myself to Sam or helped
him to better understanding of my affairs.
We were partners, with all we both had
staked in our little printing-house, and I had
dropped into that place when I came back
because it was the first thing that offered.
When Sam had·given me a thought, he went
on : —

" Poor Keene, his profligacy was absolute drunkenness. We came here to start the paper together. I did n't know as much as I do now. I had been rubbing around at different jobs four or five years, trying to study law and one thing or another, without enough money to live on, and dabbling with newspapers all the time. In six months Keene had us sold out, and he was in the gutter. So I tried it again alone. He was as bright a fellow as you are, but he could n't be kept steady. We opened the new grave-yard with him just before you came. He never did a more distinguished thing than plant his carcass on that slope. We made an occasion of it, like laying a corner-stone. Poor Kate! He left her without a cent in the world, and without a relation except this half-aunt. I should say she was literally on her wits; and she needs them, to get on with Mrs. Jutberg. Jutberg is a Swede, well-to-do, but probably the most regretful Swede that ever was in a hurry to marry an American woman. I never saw him do any-

thing but follow his wife submissively into
church.   But she has religious ecstasies, and
they tell this story of him : One night he sat
watching Mrs. Jutberg in disgust while she
paraded the aisles shouting, ' I want to be a
burden-bearer!' and the next morning he
refused to carry any coal into the house for
her.   ' Get on to dat burden yourself,' Jutberg says.   ' You vas so sveet on burdens, I
let you bear dat one.' "

Any but homeless men might have entered Mrs. Jutberg's sphere apprehensively.
The two or three weeks I had camped in
the office with Sam separated me from my
former life, and the square, roomy house
typified a return to civilization.   From the
porch inward one was impressed by exquisite
rigorous housekeeping.   An odor of roses
sifted about.   There was not a speck of dust
on the furniture or on the framed hair-flow-
ers and ancient sampler-work in the parlor.
I wondered if the orphan Kate Keene held
levees of youthful people in this little salon.
She was nowhere to be seen, and neither was

there any visible servant. Mrs. Jutberg received us with brisk dispatch. She was a small woman, of excellent trim figure, though I thought her sallow face a sullen one. Her teeth were large and broad. With unusual scrutiny I detected a looseness about the lower part of her face, which seemed thrown on its own support. But when you are predisposed against a person, and find that person a quick-footed and capable domestic angel, small minor imperfections go for nothing. Our rooms had the sweetness of lavender in the sheets. My box of books had been opened and arranged on standing shelves by some one who knew their value. I had a comfortable feeling in the house, such as I thought I should never have again in the world.

Sam and I sat down in state with the Swedish host in the dining-room, and the hostess herself served us.

" Good - evening, yentlemens," he said, holding knife and fork upright in his fists ; and I thought he was a dear blue-eyed old

fellow who would appreciate sitting and
smoking in silence with a companion after
meals. Sam gormandized on broiled prairie
chicken and talked all the time, but the
fragrance of the tea floated Mr. Jutberg and
myself into a smiling, unspoken friendship.
It was a meal to set a man on Mount Olym-
pus, Sam said, becoming heartily solid with
Mrs. Jutberg, who appeared distrustful of
the praises of men's mouths, yet exacting of
appreciation. It did indeed mark a new era
after bread and cheese and restaurant stuff,
and there was no restraining the vigor it put
into Sam. He rushed forth, as soon as he
rose from the table, into the dusk streets,
where the kerosene lamps were yet unlighted,
to further cultivate the influence of woman,
or pursue patrons for advertising, or talk
his kind of politics, or continue what he
called hustling along the development of
the town.

I was used to Sam's desertions in the evening, for we never went in the same direction
if we walked, and often I lighted a lamp in

the office and read or wrote, beetles and evening street noises buzzing up from the sidewalks. The discipline on the sanctum benches made me look forward to a bed with gratitude that astonished me, and the very best preparation for such bliss seemed a smoke on the porch with Mr. Jutberg. So we sat down, with our feet on the top step, he and his pipe, and I and one of my treasured cigars.

" I vas not a feller dat talk much ven I smoke," remarked Mr. Jutberg before each man sunk into his own sweet trance ; and I responded, " The same."

His gentle Swedish monotone was more soothing than his tobacco. The sky seemed to let its stars down almost within reach, and over eastern hummocks we could watch the unobstructed rising of constellations. There was no light in the house except in the kitchen, at the end of the hall behind us. We could hear the tinkle of dishes being washed and set on shelves, and by turning our heads could see Mrs. Jutberg and another figure passing back and forth. I wondered if the two women of the house ate in secret, and like the priests of the oracles performed their feats by hidden machinery? After my life of fierce and sickening passion these saltless doings were infinitely peaceful.

There had not been an audible word spoken in the house, when the clamor of a shrew began, almost lifting Mr. Jutberg and me, like a powder explosion, from the top step. He turned toward me, pipe in mouth, his face drawn back in apprehensive horizontal lines. I began a Latin quotation under my breath, but the terrible words of that incensed woman could not be shut out. Her voice soared and spread, and must have filled the air for several blocks. I have heard hysterical cries, but never anything so like the shrieking of a human beast. The mire of Billingsgate market and its red-faced fishwives at once came into my mind. Could any one have imagined this trim, pleasant-spoken, and skilled American woman was such a devil? The opinion of neighbors was no check on Mrs. Jutberg. She called her young relation names. The insanity of her anger being restrained by nothing but religion, she doomed the poor girl to fire and flame, which is the second death and a well-deserved one.

I saw a figure dart across the lighted space with its hands over its ears, and Mrs. Jutberg pursued it. It was then that her shrewish face worked in a spasm. The muscles struggled ineffectually while she chewed air with dreadful mouthings and contortions of the countenance, and beckoned to us with imperative hand. I leaped up, convinced that the woman was in a fit, but Mr. Jutberg shook the ashes deliberately out of his pipe.

"It vas notting but her yaw come unyointed," he explained in gentle monotone. "I put it up again. But, by Vashin'tons and all dem big fellers! it vas better out of yoint dan it vas in."

The girl's hand was stretched forth to

help Mrs. Jutberg, but Mrs. Jutberg slapped at it. My friend arose, straightening his stiffened limbs, and went in to the rescue. At my distance I thought I heard a slight click which might signify that his surgery was effectual. Mrs. Jutberg worked her jaw up and down, recovering command of it; and then, without a word to acknowledge his services, she turned her back and went into darkness at the rear of the house. We heard a door slam. Her husband took his hat from the hall and passed me, with an apology for our interrupted smoke.

"I yust valk out behind her aviles and keep her in sight. It make her so mad ven her yaw come unyointed she not stay in de house aviles, but go out and valk de streets in her sunbonnet. Seem like ven I put it up she blame me because it come down."

I shared Mr. Jutberg's feeling of uneasiness and responsibility because Mrs. Jutberg could no longer bear to be in the house with us. The long streets, safe though poorly lighted, would lead her past much jollity and

banjo and guitar playing. Nearly everybody was young and happy.

I thought it a pity that Protestant
churches never keep open doors for weary
and passion-tormented souls, as the Catholic
church does. Toilers who left their work
for a minute's prayer in the cathedral were
a common sight abroad; and the dim light
and holy silence must have done a lurid
spirit like Mrs. Jutberg much good. There
was a wide sprinkling of variously housed
denominations all over town. Every man
had put his hand in his pocket to help the
churches, and none more generously than
the banker, Mr. Babcock, until he called a
halt with sudden thought.

" Look here, boys! We 'll have the
preachers of all these churches to keep by
and by. Let up on subscriptions. We
won't build any more."

I had smoked out my cigar and thrown
the stump away, when it occurred to me
what guileless people these were to leave
their young relation alone in the house with

a stranger. Ashamed of the thought because it was un-American, I rose to go to
bed, when we met in the hall. The young
girl was carrying a lamp. There was no
back stairway in the house, I understood
afterwards, and the kitchen lamp was the
only one she was allowed to make use of.
It was clean and bright as the flambeaux of
the wise virgins, showing her face and brown
hair, and her black dress, short like a little
girl's around the ankles. She was lithe and
long-bodied, with an undulous motion as she
walked, which struck me as the perfection
of young grace. I did not expect to find
anything perfect in Mrs. Jutberg's relation,
though I was as indifferently sorry for the
lot of the unprotected creature as I could be
for anything.

We stopped, — I to give her the right of
way up the stairs, and she in humility to de-
cline it. The sickening shame which the
young experience when their guardians de-
grade themselves made her avoid my eyes.
I knew instantly that one of her ideals of

life was high breeding, — daughter of a drunkard and niece of a scold!

I said, "Good-evening," and she answered, "Good-evening."

"Adams, one of Mrs. Jutberg's boarders," I mentioned, to quiet any misapprehension.

"Yes, I know."

"I'm going upstairs too. Shall I carry the lamp for you?"

She gave it to me; but with a touching swiftness which moistened my own eyes, she turned against the stair-side and burst out crying.

"Oh, come, now," I objected, "don't do that."

I looked around and set the lamp on a step. It threw our shadows across the narrow passage, but I put my length in front of her as a screen from the street. Her slim sides expanded and contracted with the effort she made to hold her sobs. That helpless crying into which a visibly brave creature fell cut me up. I did not know how to comfort her; but I could have brought her Mrs. Jutberg's jaw on a salver.

"Never mind," I said; "I don't believe anybody heard but myself, and it makes no difference, anyway."

The girl began to laugh, and lifted her head, though tears ran down her clear cheeks. "It was n't that."

"What was it then?"

"Oh, you look like my father — you look like my father!" She flung herself against the stair-side and sobbed again.

This was flattering to a man who had had some measure of success: I looked like a sot, the opener of the new cemetery, the mortuary corner-stone, so to speak, of Trail City. I passed my hand through the thin layer of hair on my cadaverous head, being unable to hit on any suitable response.

Her second fit of weeping was short, and she dried her face, showing the freshest innocence I had ever seen on a human countenance. The guilelessness of childhood was supplemented by something like a high spiritual brightness which gave her an intent and all-alive look. Among chance comings of children into this world, I divined, whatever her parentage had been, that hers was a happy chance. She attracted the material needful to make her life.

"My father has only been dead a few months. I haven't got used to it yet."

"He left you here, did he?" I remarked, making a case against the man I resembled.

"Only until I am eighteen. After I am eighteen I may go where I please."

"He made that provision for you?"

"He only told me to stay until I was of age; and I will do as he told me."

"Perhaps he thought you would be taking a husband by that time."

"No, indeed. I am never going to marry. My father told me not to."

"He was a man of sense," I admitted, feeling more reconciled to the resemblance.

"He was the best man in the world. Other people have bad faults, but he had

only one little weakness. You don't know
what my father was to me. I miss him" —
She stopped, catching her lip in her teeth.

The forcible reminder which I had been
of this good man for the first time suggested
itself as an advantage. A differentiation,
impalpable as air, set the child apart to me,
and gave me some hold on the only friendship I felt moved to seek. I was possessed
to let out my story, which had cost lying
to keep from American ears, to a person
I had talked with five minutes. Sam had
labored on me incessantly, and closed me
up tighter all the time ; and for backing he
had our college years. This girl was not
acquainted with my kind of grief. It was
in fact unfit to mention to her. You knew
by instinct she was the species of innocent
who might stand in the thick of intrigue
and never see it, keeping company with
holy angels all the time. But I felt sure
she could help me with my intolerable load
just as she defended her father's little weakness.

I took up the lamp and rested it on the flat newel, detaining her when she would have continued up the stairs.

" I wish you would sometimes call me father. Not openly, I mean — but sometimes. I had a child of my own, and he died. I think of him day and night, like a woman."

" But where is the child's mother? "

" That is what I have asked myself a great many times," I said deliberately. " ' Where is the child's mother? ' And the only satisfactory answer I could ever give was, ' Damn the child's mother.' She left her little sick boy with me, and she left me because she had impoverished me. But the boy, he was old enough to call me father, and I should like — to hear the word once in a while."

My young confessor took hold of a narrow ribbon and drew a packet out of her bosom, her wide and solemn eyes transfixing me while she prepared to exchange confidences. From the packet she unfolded a paper, and gave into my hand her father's last will and testament. I read it by the lamplight.

Kate, my child, you are the only thing that excuses me for ever having lived. I want you to make a success of life, my girl. Do it for me. Cover my failure. Don't idolize anybody, Kate, but be friends with all. Be cautious about men; some of them are worse even than I am.

It's a battle, my child, getting through the world. The people you see best off have their fights as well as the rest of us. But if you get through with credit, think what it will be to your mother and me. For God's sake, Kate, my love, do your best; and if they let a fellow out on the other side, I will watch you night and day. Your

FATHER.

I gave her back the paper, and she folded and returned it to its place. By one impulse we then shook hands, feeling that we had made a compact of friendship.

She said, " You may call me Kate."

I said, " My name is Seth."

We stood with our eyes cast down, as became the importance of the moment.

" Well, good-night," said Kate. " Good-night — father."

" Good-night, Kate."

I gave her the lamp and turned again to the porch, where I sat until Sam came home.

II

ON THE WEST SIDE.

FRIENDSHIP between man and woman is so little tolerated or understood in our country that I avoided giving Trail City any occasion to call me Kate Keene's suitor. She herself had an instinct against lovers, so singular in a maid of her age that it was talked about. But she had an equally strong instinct for comradery, and every soul in the place was bound to Kate Keene by some invisible cord.

In the dark of every morning I heard her slip downstairs to begin her daily tasks. How hard these tasks were I do not know, the domestic machinery never appearing, though for a fortnight after our compact I had mere glimpses of her. I took to selecting books from my shelves, and leaving them with the conspicuous appeal " Read " on my table. They might or might not be appropriated by Mrs. Jutberg. But the venture proved lucky, as a small marker lettered "Kate," forgotten in one of the returned books, convinced me.

Autumn glooms and howling winds came on. The sodden prairie was raw and horrible, worse than a steamer-deck in a fog. Above seas of black and waxy mud rushed a river of wind, drowning human hope. In this bleakness everything took a trivial and contemptible guise. One said to himself, "What are these fools doing out on an open plain? Why don't they hunt shelter?" My life hung so torpidly on me, I thought every day of suicide. If there was ever man or woman born into this world who won through it without feeling sometimes impelled to take the old pagan short cut out, that man or woman must have been a stupid brute. Like the sender of anonymous letters, the incipient suicide is often the person you least suspect. I did my work; and my daily bread was something to be thankful for. But the dead level of that plain and its pursuing blackness were too typical.

On some days I could not put out of my mind a sodden and neglected little grave in a foreign churchyard, undecorated by the beaded flowers and wreaths and crowns which defied weather and memorialized grief around it. A farmer leading his freckle-nosed boy by the hand was a taunting reminder that some wretches are denied the commonest comforts of the commonest lot.

Then I began to think of winter rime on European villages. Paris, London, Rome, Florence, called me, with all their art treasures, all their variety of life in which a man might lose himself. Homesickness for things American passed into astonishment that man is held to his own place on earth by a cord he cannot break even in a migratory age. His life seems kneaded into that land, and he longs for it when he is away with a reasonless passion that has nothing to do with its adaptability to his physical health or the building of his fortunes. But

I was too poor to turn eastward again. The petty treadmill of a country newspaper had me for its automatic motor.

It was surprising to see what interest Sam took in the thing. Nothing pleased him better than leading a crowd of old rattlesnake fighters in to see our type; and when we hazarded a small steam-plant in place of the old hand-press, and began to feel our way to a daily, he was as wild as a Pottawatomie.

The whole town rushed like a comet along the plane of improvement. Its local political spirit was intense. The salary of mayor and aldermen was fixed rigidly at fifty cents per head a year. When a man was nominated for one of these offices, however, he poured out his own private means like water on the expenses of an election rather than suffer the odium of defeat. The town had contempt for any one who failed in any way to " get there."

Feuds and cross-purposes existed, but these were all new and swiftly changing, like the clouds over the prairie. No families had hereditary enemies. By the time Sam had me adjusted to the fact that Colonel York and Mr. Babcock were in a furious tug over grain elevators or the placing of the school funds, they had passed again through the amicable process which he called kissing and making up. We had to steer our bark very carefully among breakers, and lean to this side or that with discretion ; but Sam had the discretion and did the leaning.

Many good fellows thought I was sickly, and came into the office to cheer me up. One jolly, roseate old rascal, with tufts of hair like wool above his ears, swapped daily jokes about his nomination for county coroner.

" You 'll give me employment if I get there," said he.

" But why do you want to sit on such objects as I am ? "

" Well, I 'll tell you, editor : my aim is to get into some business where there won't be any more kicking. Now, the man I deal with as coroner won't kick : he can't. His friends won't : the State pays the expenses. I 'm getting on, and peaceful, soothing employment like this is what I want for my old age."

Sometimes the conviction stung me that I was wasting my prime in this eddy, with people whose thoughts could never be identical with mine. "It is not my place," my soul said. Every morning when I rose, the sickening distaste swept over me. And a man who submits to disadvantage maims his own spirit. Yet there I lay prostrate, like a tangled horse, who after vain efforts to rise sinks flat, with his head on the paving. And suppose I did stand on my feet once more, for whom should I do anything ? All around were men with set faces and tense purpose, their eyes fixed on better futures for their children and an old age of plenty. I could work with mechanical execution, but not as a creative mind.

Blessed is that transcriber with electrical touch who makes his page crackle and sparkle at the very points where we might

blindly miss the meaning. So much that
happens to us seems not worth setting down.
I have tallied these blank days as they were
tallied against me. I simply lost them without living. Sallow northern light fell across
my page while I wrote, and rain drove
against our office windows. Esther, our
periodical scrub-woman, progressed on her
knees as far as my chair; and when I had
to move, her infant nephew, whom she called
"buddy," — a contraction of "brother," —
always improved the opportunity to get on
my lap. She kept him very clean, and of
this I was glad, on his adoption of me. The
smell of dirty little boy on a wet day sur-
passes every other rankness. His pet and
constant follower, a sand-hill crane of bluish-
gray plumage, would stalk after him and
stand beside the desk, stretching himself up
to overtop me as I sat, or stooping deject-
edly to forage in the waste-basket. Esther
told me she had sometimes seen cranes dancing real quadrilles at the edge of a slew;
and the stately manners of this one, whose

name was Jimmy, testified to some breeding. But he had been caught young, and deprived of courtly example at the very time when lank leg and neck were developing to the utmost, so he lacked the wild grace of his ancestors, and knocked things over with his feet, and convulsively tried to swallow whatever he could pick up with his bill.

Seeing that I regarded Jimmy without the animosity which was so often his portion, Esther explained : "I named him after my brother that was consumpted and died. My brother used to go steppin' around slow, with his hands in his pockets, somethin' like a crane. Jimmy is a comfort to me, if he does dirty the floors and chaw clothes on the line. It takes hard work to support my brother's children, now he's gone. But you ought to seen the style they used to put on. His wife had as much as seven hundred dollars left to her. I never got none of it: it come from her folks. And she did n't save a cent of that money. I wanted them to get a home. But all-wools was n't too good for them then. How that family did dress! And they went into s'ciety and spent it all. Now she's a widow, with five children for her and me to keep, and she can't do much."

" Were you never married yourself, Esther?" I inquired.

" Oh, yes," she responded cheerfully, lifting a liver-colored face in which pleasant eyes were set, " two or three times. But nary one was any account. So I turned them off, and took in my brother's folks."

Jimmy the crane, having begun hopefully on a ball of twine in the waste-basket while Esther talked, now caught her eye and repented. He offered no resistance to disgorging when Esther picked up the remainder of the ball to unwind him, and she on her part brought link after link of cord from his midst, until it seemed that Jimmy's intestines were being spun forth through his open bill. Having parted with the end of the twine, — which I pressed upon Esther's acceptance, as we no longer needed it in the office, — Jimmy shook his wings, and uttered a resigned plaintive sound which might be interpreted " Koort."

"Jimmy's a great hand for string," remarked Esther; "and he miscalculates about what he eats like folks miscalculate about other things. Folks does a heap of things there ain't no need of. My mother, she used to part us children's hair on the side instead of in the middle; she said she wanted to save the middle partin' till we was growed, so it would be new and nice. But now it ain't the fashion for women to part their hair at all, and I might as well have saved myself from bein' laughed at so much at school. I think about these things sometimes when I 'm unwindin' Jimmy, and I wish everybody was as easy to manage in their innards."

When I told Sam this adventure of Jimmy's he exploded with a similar wish regarding my unmanageable and unseen interior. I was a trial to him at that time, sulking in retreat while I should have identified myself with the Dancing Club, the Billiard Club, the Lyric Club, the Wilderness Club; for club life began early to mould the society of the ambitious town. The Tennis Club was temporarily suspended until summer should again permit nets to be stretched and courts to be marked out. I heard even of amateur plays which outdid traveling barnstormers in the little theatre on the west side.

Nor did I take that interest in funerals which Sam, who mourned departed friends with policy and devotion, would have had me take.

"Man, you act as if you thought you'd never die. How would you like to have people slight your funeral?"

"What difference would it make to me?"

"It would make a tremendous difference to me whether folks came to mine or not," declared my partner. "I'm setting my stakes for a regular boom when my turn comes. It often brings the tears to my eyes to think how I shall be mourned and shan't be there to see."

I thought it likely Sam would not be disappointed of his boom, when I saw how Trail City packed a house to which he dragged me where an obscure dead citizen lay. The hideous drenching weather had passed, and silver mists and burnished frostiness now made the morning landscapes glorious, so that to walk abroad was a delight. Yet this did not account for the hushed multitudinous gathering. I had before seen all Trail City on the old Pottawatomie road leading to the cemetery, bearing through sheets of rain and deep mud-ruts some old shell of a body that was really no loss to the community. But at that time I had not learned the great neighborly heart of an Illinois town.

I saw Kate Keene's hat and jacket beyond us in one of the crowded rooms, and they made a spot of living interest for me while the minister's voice labored like a locomotive up a steep grade with the character of the departed.

"Our brother was — strictly honest. Nobody can gainsay that," he challenged.

"He had n't sense enough to overreach anybody, — hardly enough to come in when it rained," wrote Sam in a private note-book for my eye. The good people around watched him respectfully as he made record of local eloquence.

"Our brother's health, or rather his lack of health," proceeded the laboring advocate, "prevented his greatly distinguishing himself in active life."

"Too lazy to draw his breath," wrote Sam.

"His bereaved family" —

"Relieved family," wrote Sam.

"Come along," he whispered, when the wearied crowd were permitted to stir, and I would have escaped from the file. "It's the custom of this country to put yourself on review when you go to a funeral. You won't get any credit if you don't pass around and view the remains. Do you think that widow is n't jealously counting noses, and tallying against the absentees? The less she has to bury, the more fuss she wants made over it."

We duly paid our last tribute to that which had a dignity denied to us who gazed, and I confided to my partner, as we reached the sidewalk, that the occasion had been profitable in suggesting notes for his own obituary. " I will do you up something like this: ' The Honorable Sham Peevey, who deceived no one by dropping the *h*, has gone to his long rest, and we may now enjoy a little ourselves. His aim in life was to make his generation serve him to the utmost. Popularity was his religious creed. His favorite occupation was laying flattery on living men with a trowel ' " —

" Hold on; I never basted you," remonstrated Sam.

— " ' but for dead men, who no longer represented votes, he had nothing but a scalpel.' "

" Nobody saw it but his ill-natured partner, though."

" ' He was good-natured because he had a digestion proof against gormandizing. Energy he did possess, and a boundless desire to boom himself, but being constituted without an immortal soul, his chances for distinction in the next world are small.' "

" He never neglected his friends, however, and he has something pigeonholed for an emergency which may overtake his dear partner, Seth Adams. I 'll do you justice, my boy. It runs like this : 'His noble form, six feet in height and two inches in width, enshrined the most genial nature in Trail City. But he kept it all to himself. My friends, no corporation in the State of Illinois would miss Seth Adams more than Trail City if Trail City only knew he had been here. Traveled, scholarly, of a culture so sensitive that it could find companionship only in the silence of Esther's crane, what might he not have done in this community if he had only quit locking himself up in his own room ! So light a vehicle overloaded with soul will probably never again slip through Trail City without making any noise.' "

While we chaffed each other the pushing

crowd separated us, — Sam letting himself
be carried off with a man he wanted to dun,
and I consciously waiting for our house-
mate; for I might walk with her in sight
of the town after a funeral, like any other
acquaintance.

Mrs. Jutberg did not interfere with, or
direct, or in any way chaperon her niece,
varying her indifference only by outbursts
of unexpected rage. To see the girl try
to avoid giving offense, and keep to a narrow path unaided, harrowed me as it must
have harrowed any man who approved of
conventual care over girls. The protection
Kate had was nothing but brutal abandonment. The young town's innocence was in
fact her only bulwark. A dialogue which
we sometimes overheard took this form : —

"Aunt, do you care if I go to the Club
this evening?"

"No, I don't care where you go."

"But you have no objections? You have
nothing for me to do here?"

"If I had, I'd let you know."

"Yes, I thought you would. And Lucia York's party will call for me. If we are late, I can stay all night at the Yorks', and not disturb you."

"You 'd better," signified Mrs. Jutberg.

With large patience which would have been unnatural in any but a child trained in Kate's hard school, she would then thank her guardian for the privilege. I wondered where she had learned this gentle deference to elders so unworthy of it. The remarkable man who looked like me rose more and more in my opinion, as I reflected on what he had produced between his bouts in the ditch ; for as far as my acquaintance with the maternal stock had gone, I rejected it as having no part in the result called Kate.

Mrs. Jutberg certainly had times of exaltation and lightness, but she was not on speaking terms with any neighbor, and treated the world as in conspiracy against her. Several times she arraigned Sam and me for dark and deadly clippings in our paper. The most innocent and open human selfishness she translated as malign influence directed against her; and we heard her accuse Kate of plots and deep-laid schemes. She would nurse these ideas for days, and then suddenly explode them with disastrous force. I never saw Mrs. Jutberg dislocated by laughter; she came to grief through temper. Yet this self-tormentor was the most exquisite of that school of old-fashioned housekeepers who cannot tolerate servants, and make a fine art of living; and she would sit up night after night with any sick enemy. When her benevolence passed a moderate limit, however, I could see a gentle uneasiness appear in Mr. Jutberg; he anticipated a recoil, and he was seldom wrong.

I lifted my hat and fell into step with Kate Keene in the midst of the dispersing crowd. I cannot now tell what her features were like, speech or expression so mobilized them; but she affected me as the only individual in all that crowd. The best companion in the world is a woman capable of great friendship whose mind does not run to love and marriage. She had no self-consciousness. The awkwardness of late childhood was just passing like a discord into virgin harmony. And as I walked beside her the thought came over me that I too was young, really little beyond my boyhood. I was not twenty-eight years old.

"Death is made a very disgusting trial to a man by the customs we have," I said to her. "When we die we ought simply to disappear, as if dropped through a hole in the crust. Survivors missing us could then say with some respect and awe, 'He's gone under.'"

"Perhaps it will be that way for you and me. I have often thought it would be fine to have a bureau of death in every town or on city street corners, where poor wretches who could no longer bear life might drop it" —

"Enter without money, and disappear without a funeral."

"Yes; in some nice painless chemical way that leaves no traces, — the whole responsibility resting on the person, who decides for himself."

"I have had the same thought!" and we looked at each other with the surprise of meeting in a discovery.

"Do you believe it would be very wicked?" inquired Kate.

"I believe it would be very civilized."

"But many people would rush to the place in a passion of disappointment."

"And stop at the door. Only those who really needed to die would ever go in."

"I have seen times when I would have gone in," said Kate.

"You?"

"Yes. Those who feel deeply would be always at that door; my father would have been lost to me years before he was. We used to talk about it. He made a sketch once that he called 'A Death Bureau,' but he never printed it."

"I made a sketch on the same theme last week, and called it 'The Ready Door;' and if pushed, I shall print mine."

Again Kate and I looked at each other with astonishment at the family resemblance in mental states.

"Don't print it, because some one might read it who would make a ready door for himself; and after he was dead he would be so sorry. Now I am older, I can see there is danger of our turning around at the other side of the grave and wishing to come back to finish what we were made for."

"But so few of us are made for anything. We are accidents."

"No," said the girl, her voice softening; "no, father, we all mean something. But some of us are a long time finding out what. When you really know what you are here for and how to take hold to do it, it's grand to live. You can be full of joy when you are most miserable. Now I have found this out, — the preachers never told me: when you cannot stand trouble any longer, pray to God Almighty and say, 'O God Almighty, I thank you for everything, — I thank you for everything!' That takes the bitterness away, and makes you feel calm and as if you could wait and see what it all meant."

" I neither pray nor go to church."

"Church is everywhere," said Kate, "and you have to pray. You pray whether you know it or not."

Two tall boys pushed by us, with critical recognition of a girl overheard counseling prayer. Kate gave them a nod and a smile, and I did not think she noticed their grins until she said to me, watching their hulking backs, "Poor fellows, they are yet in cattlehood, and have to pray with a kind of lowing."

" A great many of us are yet in cattlehood, and have n't learned even the lowing."

" A man like you ought to have got more out of his troubles. Such as those yonder depend on men like you to do their thinking and direct their salvation. I have heard my father say that."

The family tendency toward religion, which in Mrs. Jutberg took the form of hysteria, had received an impetus from her father.

" It always seemed to me a childish thing to call on the Lord in trouble, and forget him at other times."

" Why, no one forgets," said Kate. " You can't forget. It goes on all the time, without words. When I am reading to people, I am praying with all my soul, ' O God Almighty, please let your light shine through me now.' "

" What do you read to people ? "

" Many different things." She turned her innocent face full upon me. " I am going to read in public for my living when I am of age."

This, then, was her ambition. The matter was settled, with sublime indifference to obstacles ; and my heart ached for her.

" Have you had training ? "

" Only what my father gave me. But he said I must learn housekeeping with my aunt until I am eighteen. For when you know housekeeping you have a trade to fall back on, as the Jews always brought up their children to have."

I secretly admired the Israelitish wisdom of my double, and intimated that she must not be disappointed at having to fall back upon her trade.

" Oh, I should n't mind going as house-maid or cook in a city while I watched for my chance," said Kate. " I don't mind work; it's beautiful. There's such satis-faction in making everybody comfortable. But I can do a better thing ; and my father said I must do my best."

" It will be very hard to make a place for yourself as a public reader, Kate."

" I know it will, but I shall get engage-ments when the time comes."

And when I saw her radiant patience and confidence I could not say another word. Could I tell her how nearly impossible it was, without stage traditions and training, influence, means, or protection, to enter a career so nearly allied to the actor's, that closest profession in the world? Could I show her that not one aspirant in a thousand who really gained the boards ever rose to distinction? Could I threaten her with the coldness of empty halls and theatres, and hard-hearted landlords who would seize baggage for unpaid bills?

The pessimism of a cosmopolite was so strong in me that I did some lying awake and suffering on account of the disappointment in store for this poor child, who deserved so much better of fate. I had no influence, no money, was of no use to her myself. This vicarious despondency, which oppressed me greatly, must have lasted two or three weeks, for winter had struck us with what the natives called a blizzard, when Sam walked into the office one morning and informed me that I would go to the Wilderness Club with him that evening. I remember the snow ground under wheels with a scream like little bells, and when I went to the railway stations for items the north wind blew the crystals like white dust. There was a fog over all the whiteness, —

dry, the very lacework of smoke-mist; and frost flowers and trees decorated our windows. Everything was so full of electricity that hair crackled, and a little "tic" of a shock went through you when you touched metal. It was several degrees below zero, and I had merely unbuttoned and thrown back my overcoat, though our stove simmered in red heat.

Our postal-card correspondence was before me, items gathered by rural helpers, and headed with the names of their respective centres, — "Plum Ridge," "Prairie Dog Hollow," "Rattlesnake Corner," "Big Slew," "Fidelity Schoolhouse," and many others. It gave one a neighborly thrilling of the heart to read that "Sam Cass is finishing the inside of his new house. That's right, Sam: first fix the cage, and then catch the bird."

And "Jerry Fox always knowed a good thing when he seen it. Jerry has took in another half-section. He now has as fine a farm as any in this part of Illinois."

" We regret to learn that Eli Harness's children is down with the whooping-cough, but health in this neighborhood is otherwise good, except Milton Singly's wife, who is also bedfast."

" Tade Saindon has took to Sundaying in Caxton. Wonder what the attraction is, and this neighborhood so full of pretty girls? "

And the human bitterness and envy betrayed in one which declared, " Some of the boys around here are getting too smart. Because their fathers can afford to send them off to college, the airs they put on is enough to disgust sensible people."

" Well," I said, looking up from this mass of local history, "you have been threatening me with various clubs a long while. But why Wilderness? In this bald world, where there is n't a stump and the trees are transplanted sticks, why Wilderness? "

" That 's Kate Keene's favorite word ; she named the club. And you will go in full evening dress."

" Sam, I have n't unfolded my dress coat since I left Paris."

" ' Some of the boys around here are getting too smart,' " quoted my partner, taking up a postal card. " ' Because they have been abroad, the airs they put on is enough to disgust sensible people.' "

" Airs would be lost on Trail City. You only feel sorrow for a man who has been away from it and its boom. What's the occasion at the Wilderness Club to-night? "

" Something swell. And the girls' mothers will be there to help them receive after the theatrical business. You think you're the only citizen that knows his little Shakespeare; you'll find out there's another of us. And it ends with a cosy ball, — good orchestra music. I want you to do the style for the firm; you can do it better than anybody, when you want to."

" But I don't think I want to."

" Come, old man. It's in the theatre. Parquet floored over for dancing; women there working like mad now, decorating with flags and things; and Mrs. Babcock has risked some of her finest greenhouse flowers in this zero weather. They're certain to freeze on the road; but when a woman goes into a thing, she goes in. Folks will be there — friends of the Babcocks' — from Chicago, and the Yorks have some of their people here from the East. Trail City is going to eclipse herself, and we've got to be in it with both feet."

"I have no desire to eclipse anything with my feet."

"Oh, come, Seth. This won't do any longer. It's treating little Kate Keene badly, you know."

"What has she to do with it?"

"Why, she's the star. And the whole thing is for charity, besides."

"Why did n't you tell me it was a charity scheme?" I demanded, with instant change of resolution. "That alters the matter. I'll come out for charity's sake. What does Kate Keene do?"

"Wait until you hear her. She does some

things that nobody else ever did. I told you her father was an actor before he took to drinking and newspaper work, did n't I ? "

" No, you never did."

" Well, she 's a corker when you put her before an audience. I can't tell you what it is. Sometimes I think it 's genius. She is n't pretty, like Teresa Babcock or Lucia York — but confound Keene ! why did n't he leave her better fixed ? I have often thought she would make a fine wife for a public man, with that magnetic pull."

" Somebody has set it down, Sam Peevey, that the basest men will take the devotion of the best women as a matter of course, but I never saw such a disgusting illustration of it as you are."

Sam laughed, shaking his ample flesh. But that evening I saw him shake more uncontrollably with weeping, for the hearty fellow always carried his emotions on the outside of his person.

The little theatre, with its single huge chandelier and row of footlights, was pretty with bunting and potted plants, and warm, and full. Chairs had been arranged upon the floored parquet, and here and in the two boxes and all around the walls spread a sea of faces. We saw Teresa Babcock turning her black eyes toward us for an instant, with the proprietary interest she certainly had in all young men; the York girls surrounded by a court and smiling; maids, matrons, men, children, a gathered population, humming like bees. All the girls had their mothers or other relatives to witness their social triumphs. I looked about for the sallow face of Mrs. Jutberg, and when Sam detected my quest he laughed at me for a dull sinner, to think she would trust her frail soul and anatomy in such a vortex of play-acting and dancing.

Then the daughter of the man I resembled came across the stage. Kate Keene looked like a Greek girl. How the slim creature in a short black dress that we were used to, became a supple goddess I do not know. Perhaps her father's stage traditions taught

LIKE A GREEK GIRL

her that noble draping — of silk, or wool, or cotton, it might have been snow; one was not conscious of material — which fell from her shoulders to the floor, and was bound under the breasts by a girdle. She had her hair encircled by a fillet. Her neck and undeveloped young arms were like veined marble. And I remember having an underthought of surprise that her wrists and hands were only expressive; were not coarsened by the labor they daily performed.

When her transformation had taken hold of us, we found it was more than a trick of clothing; she began to do with us as she pleased. If there were people in the audience whose prejudices she shocked by that peculiar simple dress, or who recalled her father to her disadvantage, they were found in their innermost hidings by a piercing sweetness of voice and presence that I cannot make known in words. It was a spell. None of the hollow tricks of the elocutionist broke it. She made people pass before our minds, magnifying our human experience.

She was Perdita as white as a lily. She was Cleopatra with a Greek-Egyptian face. With sudden angularity she was Betsey Trotwood chasing donkeys. She was a score of droll American forms which we recognized with shouts of laughter. She was age, youth, childhood, tears.

She left us ;. and four times, five times, six times, seven times, we dragged her back to give us the joy of living a moment longer in the mimic world. And then the town of Trail, with its guests, stood upon its feet, and shouted and laughed and cried, until I felt something break away within me. I rushed from the theatre, leaving Sam standing on a seat, blubbering and waving his handkerchief.

I worshiped her. The light of God Al-mighty shone through her. I seemed to walk among thick-clustering stars, and the constellations overhead were near enough to pull down. My trouble was gone. A returning tide of life filled me with warmth like success. There was a lambent spirit who had brought the world, the whole world, into this small Illinois town. It made no difference that I had managed affairs badly in the past: they had brought me to her; the main interest in life had been served.

I looked around the arctic expanse lost in the vastness of unseen horizon, and loved my town. The semaphore at the railway junction threw crimson lights across the snow, and a hissing of quiescent locomotives came to the ear. Let them plough through darkness on long quest to distant cities. I myself was landed. Through all this fury of exaltation there was no definite object before my mind. I did not know what I should do; the happiness of being was as much as I could endure.

It was bitter cold, but to the outermost layer of skin I tingled with resisting heat. My overcoat was on my arm. I breasted the awful breath of the Northwest. I was rushing to the limits of the western sidewalk when a panting behind made itself heard, and I turned to see in the dimness one of the hotel runners following me.

" You 're wanted," he said, blowing on his hands and stamping. " I 've hollered at you nearly ever since you left the theatre, but you did n't hear."

" You don't want me ? "

" Yes, sir, you 're the man. There 's a friend of yours at the house that sent for you."

" Who is he ? "

" I was just to say it was a sick friend, and to tell you to hurry."

The fact of my having a sick friend made little impression on me. As far as I paid attention to the fellow's words his message was of little account. But I walked back with him, intending to look in at the hotel, where some passing bore was probably finding time hang heavy between trains. The merest acquaintances will seize on you in the name of friendship, when they have ends of their own to serve. What Sam would have called the sick-friend gag did not in the least deceive me. I expected to look in at some rubicund fellow with his feet and a box of cigars on the table.

The huge wooden hotel, mansard-roofed and many-lighted, was gaudy as a steamer in the waste of dim whiteness. That many-storied caravansary went up in fire years ago ; but I can see it yet as I stepped from the broad stone paving into the pretentious entrance, and passed vistas of billiard and smoking rooms, and the deserted long apartment which the management proudly called its saloon parlor, from which a weak piano usually tinkled.

The messenger led me upstairs, and though this was carrying the joke of the sick friend whom I expected to find in the smoking-room too far, I followed, still in the white mental heat that makes a man externally numb and indifferent. He rapped on a door at the front end of the corridor, and opened it for me to enter. A sift of well-known perfume met me. The door shut me in, and I stood face to face with my wife.

III.

WE stood without speaking. The most vital consciousness I had was of the change that had come over me, rendering me so indifferent to her presence. Her dark beauty was intensified rather than marred by what she had done. Vivid health and the very insolence of prosperity sat visible upon her. Her eye, encountering mine with resistant hardihood, swept critically down my length. She could not help that; she was a physical epicure. It was I, care-and-sorrow-worn, lean in my clothes, who winced before her.

" You sent for me ? "

" Yes. I saw you at the station this morning. I was on the south-bound train. I got off at the next junction and came back."

" What do you want ? "

She sank into the chair on which her hand rested, and said, " Sit down."

I stood. On the opposite side of the small parlor was a full-length glass, reflecting a cadaverously pale man in evening dress, hat in hand, holding an overcoat on his left arm. His features were large, but the mouth was like a woman's. He had a thin layer of blond hair on his head. His eyes, which I had always thought blue, were points of steel. I had no interest in him as a presentation of myself, except to despise his lankness and his pitiable attitude before the world and the woman who had wronged him.

She, who had been for me the romance of youth, my first voyage, my first taste of life, the woman who had done with me as she pleased without having her caprices questioned, began the arraignment : —

" I want to know what you are doing here on this miserable raw prairie."

" May I ask what concern it is of yours ? "

" I choose to know what brought you here."

" Poverty."

" What are you doing ? "

" Editing a country paper. There was a time when I could have selected my occupation, but that time is past."

The swimming nights of our young dissipation floated between us. Any human presence is compelling, but the power held by one who has been wedded to you is a spiritual tyranny which I do not believe death destroys. I was calm, and without any desire to throw my ruin in her face. She, on her part, I could see, was yielding to the strain of the old tie.

" There is some other reason for your being here. Your talents would command something better."

" My talents are perhaps undeveloped. And the place need not trouble you to the extent of sending for me to remonstrate about it. There was really no occasion for this meeting."

Her crimson mouth flattened across her teeth. "You are here on account of a — person," she accused, and for the first time I felt jarred.

"As you are evidently neither in ill health nor in need, I will say good-night. Our relation ended when you left me in Paris with our sick boy."

"You shall not blame me with the child's death. It was the nurse's fault. I have shed enough tears without being unjustly blamed. You know I was not fit for the care of children."

I wondered that I had ever thought her fit for anything except bending the world to her amusement. I could look at her without any cursing and see the tangle of erratic motives which governed her life. It was not manly to be even bitter toward a creature so slight. Her pretty selfishness I had myself fostered. We met on shipboard, during my first voyage, and I followed her and her parents, and courted her from Edinburgh to Egypt, so that the guidebook routes were full of her. Her indulgent father and mother finally witnessed our marriage and went home, and then like two prodigals we wasted my living. And all the time that rich American friend who had been her suitor hovered around us, pitying her for the shortness of my purse, until we quarreled, and she suddenly chose her lot with him. It actually seemed now the affair of another man, and I an idiot for having taken it to heart. Her trespasses were far away in a dream, as all trespasses may appear when we look back at them from another life.

" I have not accused you of being fit for anything ; and as I said before, there is no need of this interview, so good-night again, and good-by."

She threw herself against the door and faced me.

" No, Seth Adams, you are not going to leave this room yet. I have disgraced you. I have disgraced myself. But my father and mother have forgiven me, and they have hushed things up. It is n't known, among us, exactly what happened; and that other — you know he lives abroad. I shall never see him again. I don't want to." She was crimson. "I never should have behaved as I did if you had not blamed me about money. At home they never blamed me for anything. I was n't used to it. You made me wretched, and I was determined to make you wretched, and I did. But I never thought how terrible it was until I had actually gone with him. I made him send me home when I heard the baby was dead."

I put out my hand to stop her. I was ashamed. But she caught my hand and hung to it, and I loathed her touch, shaking it off.

" Clara, I don't know what you have done to me, but you have killed something in me that can't be brought to life again. Doubtless I was to blame, but I cannot be what I was before. I don't feel now as I did for months after the baby died. That 's past.

I believe I can honestly say I forgive you, but as for anything else — you are dead to me."

She stood away from the door, turning so pallid that I remembered keenly the pinched nostrils of my dead child.

" You have never cared for me, — you let me go easily, — and I — I have been searching for you."

I broke away and ran downstairs, and paused, moved to go back and comfort her, and rushed on, anywhere, to get her out of my sight. The personal charm that I had once thought so irresistible filled me with loathing. I said, " She would try it on any man." I did not believe she had been seeking me. It was her caprice to get off the train, and to-morrow it would be her caprice to do something else.

Sam found me about one o'clock in my room, burning a student's lamp, and smoking densely from a case containing my blackest cigars. Having caused a front-door key to be made for himself, and coaxed

Mrs. Jutberg not to bolt the locks, he entered at will; but no other footsteps than his came into the house. Kate stayed all night with the Yorks, when she had been given to what her aunt called play-acting.

Sam tiptoed, the floor creaking under him, and sat noisily down, giving me so determined a look of misery that I thought my secret was out. It would have to come out to Sam, anyhow, without further evasion. The next day might bring me trouble. I was in a frame of mind to expect anything. Discovery could no longer pain me. I had a steady front fixed for Sam, but the poor fellow stretched himself out in great weariness, declaring: "You have the only level head in the firm, after all, old man. Here you sit smoking in comfort, and I've been bawling and dancing and eating and proposing ever since eight o'clock, until I'm a complete wreck."

"Lucia York or Teresa Babcock?"

"Both, man, both. I've been asking 'em right and left. If Alice had n't been engaged, and the young man in attendance, I'd have given her a whirl, too. In fact, there's hardly a girl in Trail City that I haven't proposed to to-night."

" You must have been drinking."

"Not in this town.   I'd like to get drunk."

" And which of these young ladies may I congratulate ? "

" All of them, man, all of them. I'm not quite unanimously accepted, but I'm taken on probation and the approval of our elders by one or two. And the only one I'm head over ears in love with I did n't dare tackle at all." Sam heaved a sigh which might have alarmed the house. "That's Kate Keene."

I transfixed Sam with an eye which arrested him in the midst of his emotions, and pushing the cigars toward him, I began and told him my own story.

We smoked until three o'clock, and he gave me copious advice. He had been sure I was hiding something from him. I had to defend my child's mother, so scathing and contemptuous was his wrath.

"If we had both of us come to these prairies from college, instead of trying experiments or loping off to Europe, we might be rich men now. As it is, your prospects are ruined, and mine have been damaged at least ten years."

"I like your material view of things," I said. "I hadn't quite reduced the matter to dollars and cents before, but your calculation is a great help to a man."

Sam spouted forth a strong oath and struck the table with his fist. "Everything in this world has to stand on a basis of dollars and cents. You are like a dog chained to a post, if you have n't dollars and cents. Money is liberty, freedom of choice, power, generosity, virtue, religion."

This estimate of his struck me a convincing blow in the face next morning when a telegram was handed to me, signed with my wife's initials: "I am going back to him. Shall sail Saturday from New York."

"Sam," I exclaimed, starting up from my office chair, " I must have a hundred dollars before the train goes north."

As I crushed the telegram into my pocket my partner answered, " Bank won't be open ; and we have n't a hundred dollars on the right side of the balance, anyhow, collections have been so slow."

" You must get it."

The keen north wind made me bow to encounter it as I rushed to my boarding-house. By the time I had put some things in a valise I paused. The old habit of guarding the woman I had married from her impulses had sent me like a bolt from a bow. But why should I attempt to restrain her now? What would it mean if I did restrain her, except an assertion of rights which could never be resumed? I smoothed the telegram on my knee and gave it a second reading. It had been written on an east-bound train, and sent from a station in Indiana. It dared me to let her plunge again into that life from which she had

recoiled. It was desperation, defiance, chal-
lenge. Her father and mother, ignorant
of her change of destination, would not be
able to check her. I clenched the telegram
and threw it across the room. Very well.
Let her go. What affair was it of mine?
It had now become her father's affair. Let
him see to her — I would telegraph and
warn him. But how could I open commu-
nication with him? The whole business
turned me sick. How bitter it is to feel
responsibility and loathing! To what good
did it tend, this appalling tangle of human
lives?

I had never been in the house at that time
of day before. It seemed very still, like a
sanctuary, from which Mrs. Jutberg must
be eliminated on some errand. Presently
a singing voice sought through the lower
rooms, for what I know not; but it found
me and turned me as soft as a child, so that
I wept face downward on the table. A man
in my position could never meddle with that
crystal simple spirit called Kate Keene.

She who had stood in a large transfiguration like the spread of wings, with a community at her feet, was now moving about the house again in her short black dress, forgetting her power in domestic service for us. Meaner women would have been posing for homage, but she served, served always.

Oh, I had made a mess in my boyish folly, cutting myself off from the real things, and mixing with lives I had no warrant to touch. My wife's case against me was as bad as my case against her. If that telegram had come from Kate Keene, I would have followed her on my hands and knees.

Sitting down calmly at my office desk again, I told Sam I should not want that hundred dollars.

"But I 've got it!" he exclaimed, elated.

"Take it back, then. And thanks, old fellow, for your promptness. But I 'm not going."

"What was the row, anyway?"

I opened the telegram, which I had picked

up to destroy, and, smoothing creases, passed it over to him.

He whistled, and tore it into the waste-basket. " I should think not. Were you such a fool as to want to run after her? Where do you expect to land?"

" She was my wife — and is yet."

" She 'll get unhooked from you easy enough. That kind always do. They 'll have their way if it bursts up the universe. Let her go and be hanged. Blast such business!"

I looked up at Sam, and he dropped the subject, fingering some bank-notes which he took out of his vest-pocket. His quizzical smile dwelt on me.

"Like to know who I held up? Old Billy, the coroner. He was flush, and going to deposit when the bank opened. I touched him about the boost we gave him in election. Say, Seth, my mouth has been watering for one of these new sewing-machine-looking things they call typewriters. Think what an attraction and boom it would be in this office. The fellows over at Caxton would lie down and die if they heard we had one."

" But we have n't the money for it."

" Yes, we have ; here it is. I fixed old Billy up with a note for sixty days, at legal rates ; and money loans outside at ten now. We 're solid with old Billy. It was an accommodation, but he said he would n't want it until the note comes due."

" We have another payment to make on our press in sixty days."

" But our circulation 's growing. If we get hard up, I 'll renew old Billy."

It therefore resulted that we soon had a typewriting machine in the office, a thing of wonder, which Sam manipulated and streams of farmers came to see. He showed its paces, rattling the types and jingling the little bell in endless lines of senseless printing, while I worked double, making up the paper. Our friend Billy came, also ; but when the novelty of the typewriter had worn off, his attitude used to disturb us. He would sit leaning forward, with his arms on his knees, gazing pensively at Sam.

" Confound it, what does ail you ? " Sam once burst out.

Billy shook his head. " I have n't said anything."

" No, but you wear a man out looking at him. What did you lend your money for, if you wanted it yourself ? "

" I have n't asked you to take up the note."

" No, but you come and sit on it right here in the office. Now will you go before I mash you with this letterpress ? "

Billy sat still, leaning on his arms and looking at Sam, waiting for his note to mature.

" Blast an accommodating man that repents ! Go out and wreck a train, Seth, and give the old fool something to do."

Then Sam would put on a stoic front, and fix Billy with fishlike glassiness between intervals of work.

So it came to pass that at the end of sixty days we renewed other notes, but paid old

Billy's, though with the unflinching frater-
nity of Western men he and Sam remained
in that state of mutual affection which they
called " solid " with each other.

It was not so easy to keep solid with the
social element of Trail City, for we had
started our daily, and were obliged to watch
with incessant vigilance all municipal ebb
and flow. While no hostess wanted to blazon
her social functions, and affected much reti-
cence toward the press, each was indignant
and sometimes revengeful if not blazoned
according to her full merit. I learned also
that there is no stickler for etiquette like
your small-town woman who has read and
not traveled. It came to me like another
revelation that rich men are really the scape-
goats of the poor. I saw the financial sins
of a whole community piled again and again
on the few who were able to bear them.

" Confound the unsuspecting beef ! "
growled our banker, Mr. Babcock, who took
me for a confidant in his municipal troubles.
" They 'll vote for a measure that will take

the very hide off of them.   Then as soon as
it begins to hurt they bellow and lie down;
and we other fellows, we have to step up
and do the pulling."

The beef, on their part, were wise in the
use of money not their own, and full of sug-
gestions to those who had it.   "Babcock
and York," remarked one of these small tax-
payers, "is belly-achin' and chawin' the rag
about somethin' the whole time.   If I had
as much as they have, I'd make a handsome
gift to the town, f'rinstance a lib'ary."

Sam showed his athletics in our local col-
umn, and polished off items in the prevail-
ing manner.   We chronicled the visits of
Miss Callie Van Voris, one of Trail City's
fairest daughters, to Veedersburg, or the
arrival of a lovely brick-top blonde from
Caxton.   And we announced that Mr. Blue
Thompson had accepted a position in Davis's
drug-store, when everybody knew he had
been hanging around all winter for a job.
In the same spirit, a few weeks later, Mr.
Blue Thompson being kicked out of the

drug-store for incompetency, and obliged to
fall back on his relations, we said he had
severed his connection, and would visit a few
weeks at his grandfather's, to recuperate his
health. Nobody but a political aspirant of
the wrong party had the truth printed about
him. We chronicled Christmas trees in the
various churches, and Reverend Spindle's
apt remarks to a giggling school on the
difficulty of Santa Claus's making a way
through drifts that year.

As spring opened, every stick or stone of
improvement which took shape in Trail City
we duly recorded, with glorification of the
public-spirited improver. At the same time,
having our yearly railroad passes in the
bottoms of our pockets, we performed that
gymnastic feat which Sam called jumping
on the companies with both hoofs, demanding suitable station buildings for our growing town. The penurious policy of sticking
old sheds together with new paint was held
up to Trail City's delighted ridicule.

This applause, however, was the last unanimous voice heard in Trail City that spring; for we of the North Side were growing bitterly jealous of the South Side. It blossomed, and throve, and flaunted. We sneered, and called it the Capitol and Nob Park; while it retorted jauntily by giving us the name of Chew-the-Rag or Grumblersville. But none of these little localisms crept into the paper. On the contrary, Trail City's daily organ trumpeted the vigorous solidarity which was making us the envy of all less prosperous towns.

Then the first warm day of spring, like a stroke of summer, prostrated us. One hour it was March, bleak and howling, mud from bottomless slews smearing revolving spokes to a semblance of chariot wheels; and almost at once the earth was fleeced with grass, it was April, the air ringing with bird-songs.

The blood started anew with longing which was harder to starve down than it had been during hibernating winter. I was in a passion of aching, and used to sit with hands clasped behind my head in the spring twilights, secretly demanding my own and the life I had a right to live with her. Perhaps because the riot of youth had turned to loathing, I put my idol on a pedestal and adored her, with nunlike hiding and cherishing of celestial passion. How many times I watched Kate in the April and May evenings of that spring, standing, the centre of assemblies, raying her power in almost visible streams in every direction to the remotest soul. It seemed impossible for her to imagine malice even in her aunt. Through Sam I learned that Teresa Babcock and Lucia York were always quarreling. When Teresa's betrothed from a distant State appeared to claim his rights, and Sam's engagement to Lucia duly followed, these girls agreed worse than ever. Kate used to stand between them, a golden medium through which their spiteful speeches passed gilded and refined. While they fought for social leadership, she easily led both them and their partisans, because she did not care to rule and had every one's love.

Her lonesomeness was known only to me, who drew near her in the same need. " When people see you lucky and glad," said Kate, in one of our brief talks, " they think the world must be a glad and lucky place, and are ashamed they have n't found it out for themselves. I never tell the girls my troubles. What good would it do? They could not help me. I 'm not going to make any fuss. My father said that 's what strengthens us, — bearing strains by ourselves. I love to kneel and keep still. There must be such a racket of prayers in God Almighty's ears, especially in the winter when some churches have revivals, that heaven resounds like a factory."

During this resurrecting spring she kindled ambition in me once more, and I began to work in that line which has since become my absorbing occupation. Kate was my critic. We were not often together, but I passed her my manuscript, and she set down her opinion on a separate slip of paper. It had salt sense, and was gently merciless with my faults. And no praise that ever comes again to me in this world will bring such rapture as her large-lettered " Right " penciled beside a paragraph. We sometimes disagreed and argued from our points of view, her eyes looking straight into mine with human love and experience and patience, old as the Pyramids, wise as the Sphinx. She was like primeval air blowing across the prairies, her very flesh seeming to exhale fragrance.

Clara had sent me notice of divorce proceedings from Paris. She would sometime be able to rehabilitate herself and take the place she was fitted for. Clara was one of those people who get anything they want by simply taking it at any cost. I may set down here that she finally married her friend, whose wealth was boundless, and now queens it in a certain American circle in Paris, and no doubt looks back with contempt on her advances toward me. These established facts have become a moral stay to me.

The animal instinct to better herself with-

out retrospective pangs, which Clara had,
was not understood by Kate. I left the
French paper containing notice of matrimo-
nial dissolution on my table, marked and
conspicuous, secure in the knowledge that
Mrs. Jutberg read nothing but her mother
tongue. My child was very tender with me
afterwards, not failing to call me father
when we spoke together alone. She thought
I cared because divorce was to be added to
my other griefs. Though this sweet imper-
sonal kindness might have been shown as
well to Sam, I lived on it.

Oh, what sunsets there were, flashing
across emerald plains; and twilights, beginning before the sun went down, and lingering with the smell of grass quite into
the night! The thunder-pumper began his
suction - note again in the distance, and as
days warmed and the birds thickened, like a
dream-note far out on the prairie you heard
the prairie-chicken's " bum-bum-boo." How
cunning was that lowly home-maker! I have
seen the mother hen fall, dragging her wing

and limping, to draw the sportsman away
from her nest; and, this accomplished, rise
in the air like a dart. Listening, I can hear
again, across years, the six dove cadences
which came incessantly from the cemetery
up the slope : —

"Wo - o, Wo - o, Wo - o!"

Not the least wistfulness stirred in Kate
as she saw other girls pairing off, and heard
their talk about wedding-clothes. She had
to keep clear of such entanglements. Sam,
elated by alliance with a leading house, really
congratulated himself on putting Kate like
a temptation out of his mind. He told me
broadly her father had furnished her all the
shade she could stand. What Kate Keene
now required was a rich, indulgent, and
powerful husband, a man politically established, who would give full play to her talents in a diplomatic way.

"I would like to see her in Washington,"
declared Sam. "Confine her powers to a

drawing-room, and let her work for a purpose; she could move the government."

I told Sam broadly that an engaged man
would be better employed turning his face
toward the charms he meant to admire in
the future instead of back to the charms he
had admired in the past; upon which he began a resentful and baffled eulogy of Lucia.

"You know Lucia is exactly the girl for
me. I've got my way to make. I don't
expect the old colonel to take me in out of
the wet, though a quarter section as a starter
won't go bad. Lucia York is n't one of your
fair-weather girls, either; she 'll come out
best under hardship."

"And you 're just the man for her. You 'll
keep her in hardship enough to develop all
her virtues."

"There are times," my partner said con-
temptuously, "when I would like to turn in
and be a hog myself. But there 's never
any chance; the other member of the firm
has a permanent job of it."

I pointed out to Sam how often we violate conscience and self-respect by smiling at our friends' horse-play, and suffering in accepting it as humor. But a man like Mr. Jutberg never distorted one by this passion of sympathy. He put himself sincerely into what he said, and the restricted alphabet of his native tongue drove the few words he used home in the memory.

He was smoking his pipe when an altercation took place between his wife and Mrs. York at the gate. Mrs. York, gentle to tremulousness, always fluttering about her children, apprehensive of some change in their health, must have thought of the domiciliary interest this formidable neighbor ought to have in Lucia's affianced husband. With nagging love she would coo, "How do you feel, Alice? Does your head ache?"

"No, mamma," the impatient girl would answer.

"But, Lucia dear, your poor stomach, — how is your poor stomach to-day?"

"Oh, mamma," the girls would groan, "do let our heads and backs and stomachs alone."

So, feeling her family ties extended, Mrs. York braved the tricks which fierce skylight plays with the human countenance, and dared the encounter: —

"How are you to-day, Mrs. Jutberg? How is your — face?"

"I'm well," answered Mrs. Jutberg, unmasking that face like a battery, "and likelier to stay well than folks that spend their nights dancing."

"Yes, I know you don't approve of it. But boys and girls," pleaded Mrs. York weakly, "always love the harmless amusement."

"Do you call yourself a boy or a girl?"

"Well, not exactly," hedged the gentle sympathizer. "But they like to have their fathers and mothers occasionally take a turn with them. Indeed, I feel it is only due to the girls."

"I've been wanting to ask you a question this long time," said the burden-bearer, coming nearer the fence and looking her apprehensive listener down.

"Have you?" faltered Mrs. York. "What is it? I shall be glad to answer anything I can answer."

"The question is this: What is a man thinking about," demanded Mrs. Jutberg, chopping her words fiercely, "when he is dancing with you?"

The expression of the matron outside changed at once from puzzled pondering of a conundrum to alarm and swift aversion, as she saw the other begin to gasp and chew air with inarticulate sounds.

"The man that danced with you would have enough to think about," she returned, with a tardy but effectual asperity, escaping as Mr. Jutberg sauntered to the fence and performed his usual surgery.

In a culmination of soft Swedish wrath he swore: "By Vashin'tons! I never put this yaw up again no more if it vag at every neighbor that go past. By Yacksons! I could get me plenty voman that not come unyointed at all."

Then the woman pulled her sunbonnet

over her face, slammed the gate, and set forth on one of her hag-ridden walks, and her husband looked after her, relenting. " She vas the finest cook in Trail City."

I cannot recall a word of love that was spoken by me to Kate. Yet if she came unexpectedly near, the blood jumped in my heart. Sometimes our eyes met in silence, and she was puzzling with a beneficence that for the first time held pain.

Heats like burning blasts of the desert swept those prairies in the very greenness of May. Before we could well bear the renewed tingle of life which the spring brought, that unspeakable longing for things unfulfilled, the passion of lava fires was in the air.

On a hot May night, as I came downstairs, I saw Kate in the unlighted hall. Her hand was on the newel where I had rested the lamp the first night I looked upon her face. She stood thinking, and turned mutely to give me through the dusk the smile of general good will, her potent benediction on all men. I dared to slide my hand down the rail, so near that my finger-tips kissed her dear wrist, lingering, taking joy of the touch. The strong current of her life shocked through me. The cool firm surface of flesh drove my blood like mad waters. Her hand turned and clung around mine, understanding; and then remembering, wrung itself away. Her breath was caught with a gasp. She left me, and I went out to the limits of the town, and walked and walked, feeling as if I could take the stars out of the sky and handle them one by one. How high life rose in that touch!

The afternoon of the next day, about three o'clock, night swept suddenly through the office. Our windows looked north. I was hard at work, oblivious to time, and rose for matches to light the chandelier. Then I heard a stampede of feet on the pavements below. Little pillars of dust walked like phantoms. The air which had been sultry turned deadly cold, and yet you

could not breathe it in that strange vacuum.
It was as if air had been withdrawn, and a
stifling odorless gas substituted. It rasped
all objects with a whistling scream. I saw
the sky dragging on the opposite roofs,
rising and rebounding; and running down
into the eclipsed streets, I joined men standing on a crossing, holding their hats on.
My head was bare, and I had a sensation
of having my hair pressed into my skull.
Northward, vapor bounded along the surface of the earth at right angles to a moving
wall of blackness coming out of the southwest. Ragged lights of bird's-egg green
zigzagged in this wall, and the faces of all
around me were dim and ghastly. We
smothered in an icy river of exhausted air,
and the wall came on with a million locomotive roars, crashes and screams rising in
its course. I remember Sam shouting at
my ear, but his voice was blown away, and
so seemed the people, running to cellars in
that earthquake darkness. The most dis-
tinct object in the world to me was Kate,

two or three blocks to the south, driven like a leaf.

Sometimes I dream now of swimming against eternity, clutching for the dear lithe shape I could not, could not find. The wind which drowned my voice brought hers to me. She called me. My child, my mate, mine by the kinship nothing can break — if I ever strained body and soul until blood broke through the pores, that was my instant of sinew - cracking agony. If I had found her, heaven would have made a white spot in that whirling hell.

The next thing I knew there was rain pouring down windows. I heard it hiss. Then the smell of drugs surrounded me; and I looked up into a physician's face, and at Sam supporting me, and at the ceiling of Mrs. Jutberg's back parlor. So tyrannical are the trivial things of life, I thought first of her anxious care about the carpets, and wondered what had happened to sink them below humanity.

Then I noticed that I was dressed for

bed, and had perhaps lain some time in the folding couch which held me. Mrs. Jutberg was behind my head, for she moved into sight as she came into my mind, looking chastened. But I had no further interest in her. It flashed across me that the cyclone was over, and I did not see Kate.

" Where is she ? " I demanded.

" You 're all right now," said Sam.

" Did any one bring Kate in? "

" Oh yes," soothed the doctor, " Kate was brought in."

" Was she hurt? "

" She 's well."

" I want to see her," I explained to the bland stupidity of the man. " I want to see Kate Keene. She was out in the storm. Did you bring her in yourself, Sam ? "

" I helped," answered Sam. " Shut up, sonny, and take your medicine. You were a pretty spectacle when we brought you in; must have been blown through a tree-box. What little sense you ever had has been knocked out of you for a week."

After swallowing what they gave me, I did not fully awake until it was night, and I saw the water still rushing down black panes. Sam was with me, reading beside a shaded lamp.

"Is it ever going to quit raining?" I inquired.

He put his book down, and sat on the edge of my bed. "We have had a pretty wet spell since the cyclone. How do you feel?"

I tried to move a body stiff and weighted.

"A few broken ribs," exaggerated Sam, "and a few pieces of skull jammed in."

I looked at him closely: he showed ravages himself. "Was Kate hurt?"

He twisted uneasily, and I saw he was preparing a tale for me, and gripped him by the lapels of his coat. My arms had not been broken. "Sam, you are a great fraud in some ways, but you are not a good liar. Tell me the truth."

"You idiot!" he blustered. "When half the South Side was wrecked, would anybody outside a cellar escape a whirl?

The storm cut a track of a hundred yards as clean as if a mowing-machine had done it."

"Who suffered on the South Side?" I asked craftily.

"Babcocks; everybody. But you ought to have seen how the North Side turned out to clear the wreck and house the homeless, and the food and clothes and household stuff and money they poured over the Capitol to get the nobs on their feet again. Trail City is the best neighbor in this State. There's no north, no south, no west, now; nothing but one united town."

"Was any one killed, Sam?"

"Yes: Esther's little chap, that she carried around with the crane, was blown across the prairie and picked up dead. But the crane survived."

"Poor old Esther! What did Kate say to her?"

Sam looked at me, startled.

"Kate would say something to comfort Esther."

"Well, these things have been so sudden,

none of us know how to take hold of them yet."

"She would come in here and see me, too. I want you to call her."

"I can't call her in the night, Seth. Have a little consideration."

With mad abandonment of all self-control I caught him around the neck, and pleaded by every kind memory there was between us, by every prospect he had of joy for himself, that he would have mercy on me and tell me where Kate was.

"I know she would at least come and look at me," I said. "She had love and a kind word for every human creature. If you tell me she is dead, I must bear it. But if she has forgotten me — my God! then I am forsaken."

With a blubbering cry Sam broke down and hugged me like a mother. I knew that she was dead. The pungent odor of camphor offended my nostrils, and my eyes stared at him.

"But what have they done with her?"

"Bear it, my boy, bear it. She was taken out of this house four days ago."

I tried to climb from the couch. Had I lain there a dead log and never looked my last on her sweet face? My partner had no need to force me back. I fell.

"You know how it is with me, Sam."

"Yes, I know. I've seen it all along."

"God Almighty! Sam, can you pray?"

"No, Seth, I can't."

"But you must."

"Wait till I call Jutberg; he'll fetch a preacher."

"No — pray quick. I learned one that will do. Thank God Almighty."

"What for?"

"For everything."

"Well, that's a fine prayer!"

"It's a prayer to love. Say it."

"Thank God Almighty for everything." As he spoke it, I said, "For everything," like one who lies in the trough of the sea and watches unattainable cloud mountains rush overhead.

"For everything." Kate's body was underground. "For everything." Yes, for that touch of her hand. Yes, for that cry in the storm. Yes, for the stainless love of my stainless girl. A peace came on me that passed understanding. Sam was wiping the cold sweat from my face.

"Seth! are you dying?" he whispered. "Seth, are you in a trance? Why, man, what ails you? Your face is like a spirit's."

He could do nothing but bathe my face and fan me. And as he fanned and his apprehension settled, he poured out, unasked, that chivalrous worship which men cannot withhold from their ideals. I heard his voice away in the distance, or it buzzed close in my ears. The facts struck, and I put them one by one in a vivid row.

"She was the grandest sight under white flowers that you ever saw lying with the frozen smile. The women say there was n't a bruise on her, and I don't believe she knew she was hurt. She was just caught up in the fiery chariot like old Elijah — or was it Abraham, or Moses?

"I said to myself again and again, as I looked at her, 'The Spirit of this Illinois town!' Sprung out of hardship, buoyant and full of resources, big-hearted, patient, great, — how mightily she did express the soul of the West!

"Oh, this house has seen mourning. That room was crowded with girls on their knees, as if they surrounded a shrine. And then came the young men, fathers and mothers and children. She lay in state like a queen. Near you, not ten feet from those closed doors, the pageant went on. The room was sweet with wild flowers.

"Poor old Billy and his coroner's jury, when she was first brought in, made a ring of crying men around her. I never saw such a sight before. Every fellow put his face in his handkerchief, — or, if he did n't have a handkerchief, in his hat, — and shook. To see her lying there with the dust in her hair, — who had been our pride,

— her face, that had always lighted up at meeting us, white and holy-looking —

" Billy blew his nose, and said to them, 'This is the hardest way to earn a living that I ever tried, boys. I'm doing some kicking now myself.'

" The Spirit of this town, — that's what she was; just as a beautiful ideal woman expresses the Goddess of Liberty. Pluck and genius and humility, boundless energy and vision, and a personal power that carried everything before it, — all these covered with the soft flesh of a child just turning woman, — that was Kate.

" Esther's been in to see you, Seth. She stood here, her big coarse Madonna breast heaving. She's cried her face shapeless. To top all, her brother's widow has taken the remaining children and moved back home to Indiana. 'She took everything,' says Esther. 'She did n't even leave me the crane.'

" ' We've had hard luck, too, Esther,' says I. 'But I hope we'll save our crane.' "

Before the rising sun leaped above the prairie edge far northeastward, I was wakened. Sam slept. He was not near me and could not have touched me. I was wakened by the invisible dear hand of her I love. It touched and turned and clung around mine, and the thrill of our marriage went through me, — a rising tide of life.

Two or three years ago I encountered in New York a man whom I had known as a hard drinker abroad. We renewed our acquaintance, he appearing the chastened angel of his former self. There was some attraction between us during the brief time we spent together, and I made bold to bridge years and inquire what had changed him. His name has nothing to do with this story, which, if he reads it, will forestall his pardon for setting down his secret here. I have never repeated it with my lips.

He turned himself squarely and looked

me in the eye. "Do you believe in what is called Spiritualism?"

"No."

"Neither do I. But do you believe it is impossible for departed souls to come back?"

"I didn't say that. I only meant to assert that I have no interest in spiritists, in people who live by a presumed traffic with the other world."

"Neither have I. But this queer thing happened to me. When I was at my worst, I went one night with some fellows to what they called a séance, and the woman fakir told me there was a young girl at my shoulder, and that girl made signs that she had come to be my guardian angel. The woman described her, and, my friend, I remembered the girl. She was a lovely child who died when she was about sixteen, in my native town. I don't know what interest she had in me; I was older than she was. I couldn't get rid of it. I know she is with me, watching everything I do.

Well — I would n't give up that conviction for money." He turned his cigar in his fingers and laughed.

"She takes good care of me. She does n't let me make a dog of myself any more. I would n't go where she ought n't to, I would n't let her eyes rest on what was n't fit for them to see, for anything that could be offered me. Now that is what has changed me: I 'm trying to live up to her. But I never have talked about it. She 's more to me than any living woman. Did you ever hear of such a case? Do you understand? "

I told him I understood."

THE LITTLE RENAULT.

THE LITTLE RENAULT.

AN EPISODE OF TONTY'S LIFE IN THE ILLINOIS COUNTRY.

" And a Parisian youth named Étienne Renault."
PARKMAN.

I.

THE tenth of September of the year 1680 was a day of sunshine and languor in the great village of the Illinois.   Lodges shaped like the covers of modern emigrant wagons, but colossal in size, and having an opening left along the top for smoke, filled a wide plain between river and northern bluffs.

In one of these lodges the central row of half a dozen fires had all died down to ashes except one pile of pink embers. Above it the air reeled with that tipsy tremulousness which heat imparts.   An old Indian woman sat on the side occupied by the blankets of her family, and her fingers flew like dark streaks among rushes which she was braiding into a mat — the gray-green shingle of every , Illinois wigwam. A French lad stood beside her ready to go out into the open air.

"My mother," said he, using the name as a title of respect, "you have shown me how to bind an arrowhead to the shaft; now I will show you how to dance."

The squaw, half understanding his imperfect use of her language, looked up, smiling with many wrinkles, willing to be amused by a pretty creature who avoided Indian girls and came for counsel and chat to an old woman.

He flung himself back, brandishing the finished arrow, and, turning on one foot, spun around and around at the very verge of the fires. It was like the wheeling flight of a thistle plume through the open lodge end. Outside he still whirled and sprung, keeping a tune in his throat.

Some lazy old braves were gambling with cherry stones, having spread a blanket where a wigwam shielded them from the afternoon sun. One of them shot a cherry stone after the flying, singing boy, and they all grinned with good humor at his merry defiance.

Naked children rolled on the ground, stirring up with kicks puppies as fat as themselves.

The lad skipped past a small arbor of bark wherein sat an Illinois girl and her silent lover. He checked his steps, and glanced back at them with that wistful, half-contemptuous curiosity of youth; and as he walked on lightly his flying curls settled to thick, black clusters around his neck. He had an exquisite feminine throat and face, and small, sunburnt hands. His dress was the buckskin suit of frontiersmen, yet it outlined a figure of undulations, unlike the square and masculine build of a man standing in the lodge door of the French.

He also was young, though his face had grown thin and his high temples sunken during his two years' exposure in the wilderness with the explorers La Salle and Tonty.

This Frenchman could see the whole Illinois town and the bluffs across the river. A mile or more up-stream one bold promontory jutted into the water, its glistening ribs of sandstone half clothed with cedars. This was the Rock of St. Louis, which La Salle had ordered his lieutenant Tonty to fortify. It stood waiting then, as it stands waiting to-day, for any human life which may briefly swarm over it and disappear.

Patches of cornfield around the outskirts of the Indian town had each its attendant squaw with her brood of children, driving off crows from the ripening maize. Farther away was the tribe's burial-place. Some of the sleepers were hidden from sight in the ground; but many were lifted high on platforms, with skins or blankets for their motionless palls, in sun and dew and rain, the voices of children and the monotone of the river forever sounding below them. The whole country was mellow with that afternoon light of the year which we call autumn haze.

"Runaway," said the man in the lodge door, smiling at the sauntering lad, "where hast thou been idling?"

"In the old mother's lodge, learning to set arrowheads. Has Monsieur de Tonty yet returned, Sieur de Boisrondet?"

"He is coming yonder with L'Espérance. The fathers are now settled in their retreat. I saw no hint of a monk's hood in the canoe as it came down."

As the boy turned towards the river Boisrondet detected on his face the sweet eagerness which sometimes moulds the features of a young girl.

Henri de Tonty was already striding up the bank, while L'Espérance pulled ashore the canoe they had used.

La Salle's lieutenant had at that time much to depress him. With only five followers, including two priests, he was holding ground in the midst of a suspicious savage tribe until La Salle could return from Fort Frontenac with new supplies and more men for their western venture.

Fort Crèvecœur — below that expansion of the Illinois River called the Lake of Pimitoui — had been destroyed by insurgents and deserters, its stores stolen, its magazine emptied, and a half-finished ship left to rot. Only the seed of future enterprises seemed saved in this Illinois town where Tonty was waiting on the explorer's order to fortify that great rock jutting into the river. He had first thought of pitching his camp on the natural stronghold, and setting up palisades. It could be ascended at one corner only, and might be held by the smallest garrison. But that would rouse distrust in Indian neighbors whom the French could never spare. He therefore built his lodge like any other wigwam in the midst of the town.

"You stopped at the Rock again, as you passed it, Monsieur de Tonty?" inquired Boisrondet.

"Yes," replied Tonty. A line of anxiety stood upright between his black eyebrows. His face was flushed with heat, and his cap and clustering hair were pushed back from his forehead. The ends of his mustache swept down his face. The frontier dress adorned his large presence, for Tonty unconsciously carried with him always the air of courts and battlefields.

He struck dust off the stiff right gauntlet which covered his metal hand.

"Never mind, Boisrondet. We will begin our fortification the moment Monsieur de la Salle arrives. The severest discipline in any campaign is waiting for reinforcements. On that rock you can see the country as from a cloud, except the prairie south and eastward beyond the ravine and the woods. If the fathers were of my mind they would be making their retreat on the Rock."

"And what spot have they selected for their retreat?"

"A place about a league from here, not distant from the sulphur spring. L'Espérance helped them build their lodge, and we stocked it well for them. They themselves made a cross of two unhewn limbs, and planted it beside their door."

" I do congratulate them," laughed Bois-rondet, "that they are able to make a religious retreat from these tiresome heathen. There were never two priests more disgusted with missionary work than Father Membré and Father Ribourde."

The peasant L'Espérance, stooping in gait and grizzled around the temples, flung some feathered game past Tonty's back at the listening French lad.

" Thou art young, thou little Renault," he called, " and I am old and tired. Dress these birds for the commandant's supper."

" How many times have I told thee, L'Espérance," exclaimed Tonty, turning on him, "not to be constantly shirking upon the little Renault."

" But I will dress them," cried the little Renault, snatching up the task. " It is nothing for me to do, Monsieur de Tonty."

" I am tired," repeated L'Espérance in a mutter. " The lad is ever as full of spring as a grasshopper, yet must I bear all the wood, and dress all the game, and be the squaw of the camp, and take revilings if he lifts a finger to be of use."

" Growler," laughed the little Renault, striking at the old man with the birds, " go into the lodge and lie down to sleep." And L'Espérance trotted in willingly, while around the lodge side, with the hunting spoil, trailed that youthful treble which had so often waked Tonty and Boisrondet early in dewy mornings.

The two men looked at each other with silent intelligence, and forbore to interfere. Neither ever spoke to the other about the little Renault as a girl, though Boisrondet had been present when her father put her in Tonty's charge at Fort Crèvecœur. The father was a sickly and despondent Parisian of the lesser nobles who had wedded and survived a peasant censitaire's stout daughter, and roved from trading-post to trading-post, putting his orphan into boy's attire that he might keep her with him through

all experiences. His selfish life ending at
Fort Crèvecœur, he desired to send his little
Renault home to Paris, and Tonty, in con-
sternation, took charge of her jointly with
the priests.

To Tonty she was never a girl. She was
a free and vivid spirit — pinkly clothed in
flesh, perhaps, and certainly looking through
happy black eyes, but having above everything else a tiptoe facility in dancing over
dangerous spots.

Crowded among men at Crèvecœur, she
never seemed to hear any brutal jest. The
chastening presence of priests made safer
such a place for a young girl ; yet there was
in her a boyish quality which deceived all
but her father's confidants. She had been
born to the buckskin. She had never worn
women's drapery; her round childish limbs
spurned any thought of it. The beautiful
fire of virgin youth seemed to flash from
her person. In an age when women were
pretty toys or laden beasts she lived the life
of a bird in the wilderness. The license of

a savage camp in no way touched her. She had never suffered deeply, for the early teens are kind to natural sorrow; and all visible things around her she mingled in her mind with invisible saints.

Tonty lay down on the grass, but Boisrondet still stood in the lodge door.

"It fills me with envy to see you so tired, monsieur," said the younger man.

"It was necessary that one of us should stay and guard our lodge and the little Renault," replied his commandant. "But this lying like lazy, voiceless dogs at a lodge door doth unman us. Nothing has happened since our setting forth at daybreak?"

"Nothing, except that the cry of insects in the grass never seemed so loud before."

Tonty smiled, finding in himself full response to this impatient restlessness. But even men who were waiting in the midst of negative dangers might take some delight in that mellow picture of savage life.

The river was cut by a single canoe darting from the farther bank across to the town with impetuous rush like a water-fly. Boisrondet noted it, and thought idly that some hunter must be returning empty-handed and sullen.

The little Renault could be heard caroling at the other end of the lodge while she plucked birds. Their lodge was divided into three apartments by stretched blankets, and hers was the central shrine. Tonty and Boisrondet occupied one end, and the other held L'Espérance, a forge, and some tools saved from the pillage of Crèvecœur. The servant readily yielded his fire to the necessity of cooking, but it vexed him daily to have a mere boy — the little Renault, in fact — set apart as if more reverend than a priest. The priests, look you, had not been above sleeping and teaching in the lodges of the very Illinois.

Tonty lay with his head in the grass, letting the sun dazzle his half-shut eyes, while he piled up visions of this Illinois country like those transparent clouds pinnacled in the zenith. His two years in the wilderness with La Salle had been a constantly rising tide of misfortune. But tides are obliged to ebb, and this silence must be the turn. La Salle had started to Fort Frontenac in March. He was surely retracing the five hundred leagues with supplies. La Salle could outmarch any man of New France.

They would soon fortify the Rock and make it a feudal castle to these timid savages. Neighboring tribes would gather close and help to form a strong principality. It would be easy from this vantage-point to penetrate that unexplored river called the Mississippi.

But a yell rent this structure of thought like a tongue of lightning, and Tonty bounded to his feet. Calls and cries streamed in every direction, as if the whole Indian town had become a shower of meteoric voices. The women started from their cornfields, wailing in alarm, and naked children sprawled and uttered the echo of woe. Cherry stones and the stakes won thereby were forgotten. The hunter who had crossed the river was surrounded with lamentation.

Tonty found his followers at his side almost as soon as the yell broke out. They had lived so long on the edge of peril that union was their first instinct. L'Espérance was wide awake. Tonty put the little Renault between Boisrondet and himself, and as the savage mob surrounded them he unconsciously held her with his sound arm. Little Renault's curls were full of bird down, but her black eyes were full of courage.

" What is the matter ?" demanded Tonty in imperfect Illinois.

" The Iroquois are coming! The Iroquois are marching here to eat us up."

" The Iroquois," screamed a wrinkled old warrior, " are your allies. They are at peace with all the French. They are your friends. But you are no friends of ours. Children, these Frenchmen have come here to betray us. They have brought the Iroquois upon us."

Out came the knives, Tonty with iron-handed arm pushing them back — persuading, shouting. The Indians drowned his voice with yells. The very squaws ran with firebrands. Some of the furious multitude fell upon the French lodge, and its mats flew in every direction. From the midst of falling poles ran sinewy red-bodied fellows dragging the tools and heavy forge which Tonty and his men had brought with such pains through the wilderness. The splash of the clinking mass in the river testified to their final use.

The lives of the Frenchmen standing back to back were scarcely a breath long. Tonty's stiff gauntlet kept the knives off, and he made his voice heard through the howling.

"If you kill us you kill yourselves. I tell you we are your friends. If you kill us your French father will not leave a man of you alive. We brought no invaders to your country. We know nothing about the Iroquois. But since they have come, I tell you we will go with you to fight them."

II

" FULL of intelligence and courage," as a priest has described Tonty in this strait, his imperfect Illinois made the Indians slow to understand him. But as they understood, their tense threats relaxed; and with continued lamentation they turned to break up the camp.

The canoes were pushed out and filled with women, children, and provisions. Nearly all the young braves were away in a war-party in the northwest. The three or four hundred remaining were the oldest or youngest warriors. The Illinois Indian at his best estate was no model of courage. About sixty men accompanied the retreating town to a flat, wooded island down the river, where temporary lodges could be set up and defended.

The remainder at once began to prepare

for battle. They brought wood and built great fires along the shore. Weapons were made ready, bodies greased and painted, and a kind of passover meal eaten.

The sun went down, and mists brooded on the river, but there was no silence all that night. The Illinois sang war-songs and danced war-dances under the slow and majestic march of the stars. Their fires shone on the water, and their dark, leaping bodies threw shadows across the deserted town.

Tonty and Boisrondet sat apart, also sleepless, taking counsel together. L'Espérance had been missing since the tumult of embarking. He, also, had taken a canoe and slipped away. Both masters were severe on him until they found next forenoon that he only went to bring the priests back, lest some of his faith should die without absolution.

Boisrondet had brought some of the scattered mats for the little Renault, and she hid in them as in a nest from the growing chill of night, sleeping like some sylvan creature reliant on the power that sheltered it.

Scouts sent out in darkness came back at early morning with news. They had seen the army of Iroquois creeping under cover of woods, armed with guns and pistols, and carrying rawhide bucklers. They had seen, they said, — scowling aside at the Frenchmen, — La Salle himself leading the invaders. And at that the whole camp again rushed to take Tonty and his followers by the throat.

"If all the Iroquois had stolen French clothes you would believe there were many Monsieur de la Salles coming to fight you," declared Tonty. "He does not turn upon his brothers as you do. I tell you we will go with you to fight the Iroquois."

The frenzied tribe at once threw themselves into their canoes with these allies and crossed the river.

It seemed to both guardians that nothing could be done with the little Renault except to carry her into the action. Boisrondet gave a bitter thought to the selfishness of her father, and Tonty regretted not sending her with the priests. But life in her rose to the occasion. Her moccasins moved in swift unison with Tonty's and Boisrondet's up the wooded hill and across a tangled ridge. Her buckskin blouse was scratched by briars, but she herself went laughing and rose - lipped like Diana, carrying a weapon and eager for game. It seemed to Boisrondet the cruelest thing ever done, this shouldering a child into battle with wolfish men.

Few of the Illinois Indians had guns. They were armed with bows and arrows. They swarmed out on the prairie to attack the Iroquois, who came from covert with whoops and prancings, and roar of firearms and low song of flying shaft mixed with savage battle-cries.

At the instant of encounter Tonty saw how it must go with his allies. They were no match for the Iroquois with all forces mustered, and this fragment of them began to give back even in the fury of onset.

He offered to carry a wampum belt to the Iroquois and to try to stop the fight, and the leaders gladly gave him the flag of truce and sent a young brave with him.

Tonty started out across the open field towards the smoking guns of the Iroquois with this Indian at his right side. He felt a touch on his left elbow, and turned his eyes to find little Renault and Boisrondet keeping abreast of him. He stopped and commanded: —

"Go back — both of you. Boisrondet, your orders were to take care of the lad."

"Monsieur," said Boisrondet, to the spat of Iroquois bullets on the prairie sod all around them, "the little Renault would not be kept back."

"Monsieur de Tonty, we go with you," she said.

"You will go back," repeated Tonty, meeting the living light of her eyes with military decision. "Boisrondet, pick up the lad and carry him back. Your duty as a soldier and a gentleman is to keep him out of this danger."

Boisrondet seized and lifted the little Renault in his arms. She struggled with all an untamed creature's physical repugnance to handling, and with all a woman's despair at being dragged from the object to which she clings. In her frenzy she struck Boisrondet upon his bulging forehead with no unmuscular fist.

"Go back with them," said Tonty to the willing young Indian. And running on alone, he did not see the Iroquois arrow which stooped, jarred, and stood upright in the girl's shoulder.

The young Indian alone saw it, and pulled it out as he hurried at the heels of Boisrondet, who felt his load relaxing while he panted and trampled through resin weed and yellow flowers back to the Illinois lines.

Tonty had left his gun when he took up the belt of peace. He held the wampum strip as high as his arm could reach, and

rushed directly upon the muzzles pointed
at him. His dark skin and frontiersman's
dress scarcely distinguished him from the
savage mob which closed around him, and
before he could speak one of the Iroquois
warriors stabbed him in the side. The
knife struck a rib, and made only a deep
gash instead of killing him. He half fell,
but caught himself, and opened lips from
which blood, not words, gushed first. He
held up and shook the wampum belt, and
an Iroquois chief shouted that he must be a
Frenchman, since his ears were not pierced.
This brought some about him who opened
his shirt and tried to stop the wound. But
the great howling multitude — which an
Indian army must become before it can act
as an engine of war — was for finishing
him.

Tonty spat the blood from his mouth,
and declared to them that the Illinois were
under the protection of the French king
and governor. He demanded that they
should be let alone.

One of the braves snatched Tonty's cap and waved it high on a gun. At that the half - suspended firing broke out more fiercely than ever. He urged and demanded with all his strength. A cry rose in front that the Illinois were advancing, and that instant Tonty felt a hand grasp and twist his scalp-lock. He looked over his shoulder at the fierce face of a Seneca chief; but an Onondaga knocked the scalping knife from the Seneca's hand.

Tonty was spun in a whirlwind of clamor and threats, putting his own shout against the noise of savage throats, and proclaiming that the Illinois had countless Frenchmen to fight with or to avenge them.

No one ever worked with imperious courage more successfully on the temper of Indians. The quarrel sank to his demands. Old men ran to stop the young braves from firing.

The little Renault had been docile, and walked willingly up the ridge with Boisrondet. She told him she was ashamed of her behavior and of keeping him out of the action. But she said nothing about her wound to a man who would insist upon examining it. The arrow stab in her buckskin blouse gave no vent to the blood, for that had taken to moving in a slow trickle down her back. Boisrondet, trembling betwixt chagrin and rapture, said little, but kept his gaze upon her and around her like an atmosphere of protection.

She sat down facing the firing, and Boisrondet stood by her, — on his part seeing neither smoke nor moving figures, neither dew on the turf nor distant blue strips of forest.

Two Récollet capotes moved down among the waiting Illinois, for L'Espérance had not tarried about bringing the priests. They hurried to meet Tonty. He came staggering back across the open prairie, holding up an Iroquois wampum belt as the sign of his success.

The little Renault let her restrained breath escape in a sob.

"He is safe! But he is pitching forward! He is wounded, monsieur! They have hurt him!"

She herself reeled as Tonty did before the priests received him in their arms; and a deadly sickness, the like of which the little Renault had never felt before, brought her head down among the knotty herbage of the hill.

III.

THE clear September morning seemed to stream around Tonty's eyes in long pennons of flame as Father Ribourde and Father Membré helped him to reach his allies. He was still under a nightmare, and struggled for speech to warn his weak people of the treacherous enemy who were checked only by his threats. He held up the wampum belt and told the Illinois that it was an Iroquois peace, but it would be wisdom on their part to retreat from an Iroquois peace. If they and their families withdrew down the river, leaving some of their wise men in sight of signals, he would treat with the invaders and try to induce them to leave the country.

The small army which had escaped defeat could indeed see nothing better to do. They recrossed the river to their town, and set the lodges on fire, thankful for any chance of saving their national life.

An Indian might have little sentiment about his lodge, which was only a shelter, and never contained very much besides the row of fires. If destroyed, it could be re-built anywhere with new poles and mats. But his dead, on platform or in earth, were sacred relics to him. In the fleet of canoes retreating down the Illinois River many a shaven, dusky head was turned, many a mournful eye rested on that spot which could be no longer kept, and might soon be desecrated by a wolfish enemy.

Boisrondet and L'Espérance, with the Récollet friars, set to work to repair their own lodge, which the Illinois had torn down. Here the priests gave Tonty's wound a better dressing than that of his wild sur-geons, and the little Renault lay on her blanket at a distance from him, seeking no remedy for her stiff hurt except to keep him in her sight.

Tonty had made the Iroquois pause ; but they promptly crossed the river and prowled over that great field of smoking lodges.

They took such poles and posts as had not burned, and built themselves a rough fort in the midst of the abandoned town.

Boisrondet found some blankets which he hung around the little Renault when night came. But she needed no privacy for sleep. He thought the prowling and yelling of the Iroquois made her toss, and draw her breath in tremulous starts. In the morning he was careful to get food for her, while he let L'Espérance serve Tonty and the priests. The Illinois had carried away much of their corn from the underground storehouses, but their ungathered fields still stood; and while the invaders trampled the crop, L'Esperance found some supplies for the inmates of Tonty's lodge. The little Renault awoke with fever, but that day was so full of effort and danger that the men, her guardians, overlooked her state.

They were called to a council by the savages. Tonty rose up and went with his followers into the sapling fort.

On the girl's fever-swimming eyes the

circle of hideous Iroquois faces and half-
naked bodies made grotesque impression.

Tonty sat in front of her, on each side of
him a priest. When he had to rise they
helped him; but on his feet he was like
the cliff across the river. His voice kept
respect hovering in all those glittering and
restless eyes, though a chief began the council by asking him insolently where were all
the Illinois warriors he had boasted of, and
the army of French who would keep the
Iroquois braves from eating the flesh of a
worthless tribe.

Tonty repeated the threats and demands
he had before made. Six packs of beaver
skins were laid before him. A chief prof-
fered them piecemeal. Two were to promise that the Iroquois would not eat the
children of the French — those cowardly
Illinois; a third was the plaster which must
heal Tonty's wound; the fourth was oil for
anointing all French joints present at the
council; the fifth said the sun was bright,
and it was a good day to begin a journey;

and the last ordered the French to arise and leave the Illinois country.

Tonty again came to his feet, and thanked his red brothers for their gift. But he desired to know when they themselves meant to leave the Illinois country.

Every copper-hued face turned darker; every guttural voice broke out, in presence of the pledge just made, with a declaration that their tribe would eat Illinois flesh before they went.

Tonty kicked the pack of beaver skins from him. It was their own method of expressing contempt for a one-sided treaty.

The Indians sprang up and drove his party out with drawn knives. The little Renault, hurried by Boisrondet, turned to see Tonty come last from the palisade, still restraining the savages by the threat they dared not disregard. He was determined to stand to the last risk between them and the tribe they had invaded.

During that day L'Espérance felt that he was throwing his scalp at the Iroquois by the frequent trips he made to the river, and all on account of that lad pampered among blankets, who would be constantly laving, and bathing, and drinking, for lack of other amusement.

Clean as a flower at all times, the little Renault was appalled to discover something like infection in her flesh, which she could not soak out. As the day wore to a close, her illness so increased that she was forced to look around the blanket with glittering eyes, and whisper for the help of Father Ribourde. As shy of handling as a fawn, aversion even to his touch made her face piteous.

" Father, I cannot endure any longer to be filled with sickness from an arrow wound," she pleaded in excuse for the attendance craved. " There is something foul in my shoulder which I cannot wash away."

The buckskin was drawn partly off; and though she had covered herself, the stain of shame deepened the pink of her angelic flesh as she submitted to the surgeon.

"Why did you not speak of a wound before?" demanded Father Ribourde.

"My father, I could not."

The priest's outcry brought his brother Récollet and Tonty behind the blanket, and jealously, though reluctantly, at their heels, Boisrondet. He took note of the cowering, blush-burned girl; but Tonty saw only the green-rimmed wound on the little lad's shoulder.

"It was a poisoned arrow," pronounced Father Membré.

At that Boisrondet wheeled and rushed into the open air cursing himself, and Father Membré followed close by his ear rebuking him. In many a victim the wound must have worked death within the time she had suffered, but her strong health and wholesome blood resisted. No medicine, no surgeon's skill, could now take the burning foulness out. The poison was in her eyes; it beat in her wrist and hammered in her brain.

"Poor little lad!" groaned Tonty. "I

wish I could take this from thee and add it
to my dagger cut. We have all been bad
guardians. The boy would not be sacrificed
thus if Monsieur de la Salle had been
here."

"Must I die, father?" inquired the little
Renault, lifting her eyes to the priest's sor-
rowful face when Tonty no longer stood by.

"The lives of all of us are in the hands
of God," he answered. But while he
dressed the gangrened spot he examined
her conscience, and finished by giving her
absolution.

"The only penance I shall lay upon thee,
my daughter," murmured on his priestly
monotone, "is to bear with patience such
suffering as may result from this misfortune."

He added tales of martyrs and triumphant saints to keep from her ear the stormy
agony of Boisrondet and Father Membré's
remonstrances outside the lodge.

The Iroquois allowed another night to
pass, and then ordered the French to be

gone, giving them a leaky canoe for their voyage.

Tonty had done all he could to protect the timid tribe in retreat. He saw that he must now set off up-river, so the boat was provided with some corn and blankets and the guns of his men. Already the Iroquois were busy tearing down the scaffoldings of the dead. The plain, so lately a peaceful barbarian city, smouldered in little heaps. Groups of Iroquois paused in their work of desecration to howl a derisive adieu to the voyagers.

As the canoe passed the foot of the Rock, Tonty looked up its height, hopeless — so poorly do we gauge the future — of ever planting the French flag on its summit.

IV

THE canoe was so leaky that it had to be pulled ashore when Tonty's party had rowed up-stream about twenty-five miles. They camped early in the afternoon. The two priests built a fire, while Boisrondet and L'Espérance cut branches, and with these and blankets made a couple of knotty mattresses on which Tonty and the little Renault could rest with their feet towards the blaze. Tonty's wound was again bleeding. After efforts to mend the boat he dropped upon his pallet in deadly sickness, and lay there while the autumn afternoon dimmed and faded out as if the smile of God were being withdrawn from the world.

Father Ribourde and Father Membré tended both patients with all their monastic skill. The little Renault was full of delirious laughter. L'Espérance, while he labored on the boat with such calking as the woods afforded, groaned over the lad's state and reproached himself for ever grudging the child service. Boisrondet worked at dragging fuel as if his one desire was to exhaust himself and die. As night came on he piled a fire of huge size, though it was a dangerous beacon, for they were camped on a flat and wooded strip some distance from sheltering bluffs, and their light perhaps drew other prowlers than the Iroquois. During the night there were stirrings in thickets, and once a soft dip or two in the river, as if a canoe paddle had incautiously lapsed to its usual motion.

After a meagre supper Father Membré and L'Espérance lay down to sleep while Father Ribourde and Boisrondet kept guard. The weather was changing, and a chill wind swept along the river valley. It continually scattered the little Renault's curls over her fever-swollen face, and Boisrondet, unable to endure this, built up a screen of brush. He sat on the ground beside her pallet, and Father Ribourde sat at the other side, though the priest rose at intervals and examined Tonty.

The whole pile of burning logs was heaped between the little Renault and Tonty. He lay opposite her, with his feet, also, to the fire, sleeping as only exhausted frontiersmen can sleep. Nothing in woods or stooping clouds, or in the outcry of spirits around him, reached his consciousness all that night. He was suspended from the world in a swoon of sleep. His swarthiness was so blanched by loss of blood that his black hair and mustache startled the eye. Father Ribourde listened for his breath, into such deep recesses had his physical life made its retreat.

But the girl on the opposite side of the fire brought echoes from the darkness. She sang. She thought she was dancing in a whirl along peaks, or fishing in the river with L'Espérance, or shooting arrows at a mark with young Indians, or moving across the prairie with Tonty on his errand

to the Iroquois. Through every act ran
gladness. She exulted upward through the
fire-gilt branches.

"O Mother of God, what joy thou hast
given me! If there had been no Monsieur de Tonty — think of that! Then I
should have crouched like fields blackened
in frost. Then I should not know what life
is. How desolate — to be without Monsieur
de Tonty! The savages, and the wretches
at Crèvecœur, they are all like grasshoppers
beside him. I would rather have him call
me his little lad than be queen of France."

The priest's soothing had no effect on
her fever-driven imagination. She drank
when he held a cup to her mouth, and stared
at him, still laughing. But during several
hours there was scarcely a pause in her talk
of Tonty.

Boisrondet sat behind her back — for she
lay upon her sound shoulder — and endured
all this. The flower of martyrdom and the
flower of love bloomed there before the
priest in the dank woods beside the collaps-

ing camp-fire. The lonesome, low wail of wind was contradicted by the little Renault's glad monotone. All the innocent thoughts which a girl pours out to her mother this motherless girl poured out to Tonty. It was a confession more sacred than any made to a priest. Boisrondet put his hands upon his ears.

Ruddy embers shone on Father Membré and L'Espérance, Récollet's capote and servant's shaggy dress rising and falling in unison throughout the night; for the watchers did not wake them at all.

When Father Ribourde rose up again to look at Tonty, Boisrondet crept to his place and sat by the delirious girl's head. The priest said nothing, and accepted the change. It became his care to keep the little Renault from jarring her wound with her groping hands.

Boisrondet's eyes may have pierced the floating veil of delirium to her consciousness. The smile of vague happiness which she gave the priest turned to a look of solicitude.

" Sieur de Boisrondet, did I hurt you ? " she cried.

He shook his head.

" Forgive the blow."

" I was grateful for it," muttered Boisrondet.

Still his heart-broken eyes pierced the pavilion of her gladness, and she cried out again : —

" Sieur de Boisrondet, did I hurt you ? "

" No, no, no ! "

" Forgive the blow."

" O saints in heaven ! " the man groaned, holding his head in his hands.

" How good is God," said the little Renault, returning to her heights, " who made all his creatures so happy ! My Monsieur de Tonty, *my* Monsieur de Tonty " — So she moved on through the clouds.

Tonty awoke at daybreak and stood up weak and giddy, looking first at the pallet on the other side of the sylvan hearth. A stiff small figure was covered there, and Boisrondet was stretched beside it face downward on the ground.

"The poor little lad!" groaned Tonty, coming down on one knee and lifting a blanket edge. "When did he die, Boisrondet?"

Without moving Boisrondet said from the ground: —

"She died not long after midnight."

Her face in its pillow of black curls was a marble dream of gladness. She had the wonderful beauty of dead children, and Tonty saw her as a dead child rather than as a woman triumphant in flawless happiness, whose uninhabited face smiled on at her wondrous fate. She had seen her hero in his splendor without man-cruelty and pettiness. The world had been a good place to the little Renault.

Father Ribourde had no candles to put at her head and feet, but he knelt saying prayers for her peace.

The day was chill and sullen, and occasional spatters of sleet glazed twigs and grass tufts. Father Membré and L'Espérance silently took the labors of the camp upon themselves. They dug roots to add to the scant breakfast, and brought fuel. Boisrondet made no response to priest or commandant, but lay on the ground without eating until the slate-gray afternoon began to thicken.

" Boisrondet," then said Tonty, stooping, and taking his subaltern by the shoulder, " the Indians left us not a tool, as you know. We cannot hollow out any grave which would be deep enough to keep the little lad from the wolves."

Boisrondet shivered as if he were beginning to feel the sleet in his hair and on the little Renault's blanket.

" We shall have to sink him in the river, Boisrondet. Be a man."

Boisrondet rose directly, with fierce readiness to do the thing at once if it must be done. He did not look at her again, but sat under a tree with his back turned while preparations were made.

L'Espérance brought many stones, and the priests ballasted and wound the body in the best blankets the camp afforded, tying the packet well with buffalo thongs. They placed it in the canoe, and Tonty called Boisrondet.

Both Récollets stood on the bank repeating prayers while Tonty and Boisrondet pulled up against the current. The river was a dull monster, but a greedy one, reaching for its prey through the boat's seams.

"Will this do, Boisrondet?" appealed Tonty.

"Pull a little farther, monsieur. I cannot bear it yet."

Tonty with his single-handed stroke continued to help hold their boat against the current.

Three times they pulled up-stream and floated down past the friars.

"Will this do, Boisrondet?" twice repeated Tonty. Twice the answer was: —

"Monsieur, I cannot bear it yet."

The commandant avoided gazing at Boisrondet's misery. His fraternal gaze dwelt on the blanket chrysalis of the little Renault. He would have given his remaining hand — which meant his future career — to bring back the boy's life, but even to his large sympathy Boisrondet's passion was like a sealed house. It had been impossible for him to grasp the feminine quality in that lad's black curls and flower-fresh face.

"My poor Boisrondet," he urged, "we must have the courage to lift the little lad and do for him what he would do for us."

"Lad! lad!" burst out the other with scoffing. "Always lad to you — the sweetest woman that ever drew breath!" His voice broke down, and he distorted his face, sobbing aloud.

Tonty broke down and sobbed with him. They arose with a desperate impulse together, the man she loved and the other man who loved her, lifted their heavy burden, poised, swung, and threw it out upon the water. It smote the river and sank, and their canoe reeled with the splashing and surging of a disturbed current. Tonty staggered and sat down gripping the sides of the boat, feeling his wound start afresh. Nature's old sigh swept across the wind-harp of treetops. The river composed itself and again moved steadily, perhaps rocking the packet in some pebbly hollow, perhaps passing it on towards the Missis-sippi. And the priests' voices concluded their monotone for the dead.

" Heaven give him sweet rest in this river of the Illinois ! " uttered Tonty. But Boisrondet said nothing more.

When the canoe touched the bank Bois-rondet took his gun and hurried into the woods. He did not come back at night-fall or in the morning. The others at first respected his quest after comfort. Then they searched for him, discharging their guns, and calling. Yet one more day they waited for him, the weather's increasing bitterness threatening instant winter.

When they finally broke camp the worth-less boat had to be abandoned. Each man made up his little pack of necessaries. The little Renault lay in the Illinois. Either

Boisrondet's scalp hung before some savage wigwam, or he had hidden himself to die in the depths of the wilderness. They could only take their fate in their hands — as we must all do — and toil on towards the great lake.